The Road That I Must Walk

The Road That I Must Walk

A Disciple's Journey

Darrin W. Snyder Belousek

Foreword by Alan and Eleanor Kreider

CASCADE *Books* • Eugene, Oregon

THE ROAD THAT I MUST WALK
A Disciple's Journey

Copyright © 2014 Darrin W. Snyder Belousek. All rights reserved. Except for brief quotations in critical publications or reviews, no part of this book may be reproduced in any manner without prior written permission from the publisher. Write: Permissions, Wipf and Stock Publishers, 199 W. 8th Ave., Suite 3, Eugene, OR 97401.

Cascade Books
An Imprint of Wipf and Stock Publishers
199 W. 8th Ave., Suite 3
Eugene, OR 97401

www.wipfandstock.com

ISBN 13: 978-1-62564-365-0

Cataloguing-in-Publication data:

Belousek, Darrin W. Snyder.

The road that I must walk : a disciple's journey / Darrin W. Snyder Belousek ; with a foreword by Alan and Eleanor Kreider.

xvi + 176 pp. ; 23 cm. Includes bibliographical references.

ISBN 13: 978-1-62564-365-0

1. Christian life. 2. Peace—Religious aspects. I. Title.

BV4501.2 S635 2014

Manufactured in the U.S.A.

All scripture quotations, unless designated otherwise, are taken from the New Revised Standard Version Bible, copyright © 1989, Division of Christian Education of the National Council of the Churches of Christ in the United States of America. Used by permission. All rights reserved.

Scripture quotations designated (NET) are taken from the NET Bible® copyright ©1996-2006 by Biblical Studies Press, L.L.C. http://netbible.com. All rights reserved.

Scripture quotations designated (REB) are taken from the Revised English Bible, copyright © Cambridge University Press and Oxford University Press 1989. All rights reserved.

Quotations designated (BCP) are taken from The Book of Common Prayer, published by Church Publishing Incorporated for the Episcopal Church. The BCP is in public domain.

For our children
Liam, Lydia, and Luca

Learn from Jesus,
for he is gentle and humble in heart,
and he will give rest for your souls.

*Let me hear of your loving-kindness in the morning,
for I put my trust in you.
Show me the road that I must walk,
for I lift up my soul to you.
Deliver me from my enemies, O Lord,
for I flee to you for refuge.
Teach me to do what pleases you,
for you are my God.
Let your good Spirit lead me on level ground.*

—Psalm 143:8–10 (BCP)

Contents

Foreword by Alan and Eleanor Kreider   ix

Preface   xi

Prologue: Plea for Grace—A Disciple's Prayer   xvii

The Call to Follow

1. Not I, but Christ   3
2. What Would You Do?   15
3. I Do Not Know this Man   23

The Valley of Shadows

4. The Way Home   39
5. Into Your Hands   47
6. Like Silent Human Sorrow   59

The Way of Life

7. What We Live By   75
8. For God So Loved the World   85
9. I Am the Resurrection and the Life   101

The Way of Peace

10. Body, Soil, and Spirit   121
11. Body of Christ   127
12. Jesus of Dresden   137

Epilogue: Path to Peace—A Disciple's Pilgrimage   149

Bibliography   173

Foreword

> *"I have long since come to believe that people never mean half of what they say, and that it is best to disregard their talk and judge only their actions."*
> —Dorothy Day, *The Long Loneliness*

DOROTHY DAY'S BLUNT SUMMARY ILLUMINES not only her own life, but also the life of Darrin Snyder Belousek. A growing number of people are paying attention to St. Dorothy, but it may be less clear why they should be interested in Darrin. This special book will show them why. Darrin is a Christian whom Dorothy Day would respect. He is tenacious yet teachable, rigorous yet humble. Above all he acts as well as talks; he is a disciple walking on the road with Jesus. Throughout this book he recounts his "pilgrimage to the gospel of peace in a time of war." He begins the book with questions:

> How much of myself (and my stuff) must I give up to follow Jesus? How does belonging to a faith community shape being a Christian? How do I walk in faith with friends whose faith is unclear or uncertain? What gives Christians hope in the face of power politics? Can I be pro-life and decry war, too? How do I make peace amidst the wrongs of the world?

By the end of the book's thirteen chapters his readers have learned to know Darrin. We have watched him as he answers not only by thinking but also by taking risky steps. A street beggar, a mentally tormented woman, a stranger in a foreign city—these have become Darrin's life-teachers. As he follows Jesus he has learned that he must change not only his mind but also

Foreword

his priorities and behavior. Choosing against the security of an academic career, Darrin has discovered that sessional employment and geographic moves have offered unexpected opportunities in his pilgrimage of faith.

The theology that results from his life is scrupulous, thoughtful, and earthy. Darrin offers his theology in several media. Poetry expresses his response to the obliteration bombing of Dresden; testimony grows out of his experience of community in inner-city South Bend, Indiana; meditation on scripture (the Gospel of John) illuminates the politics of Jesus in conflict with empire; philosophical rigor flashes out in his engagement with the doctrine of the Just War. Undergirding all these approaches are Darrin's bedrock convictions—that God is with us, that Jesus reveals God to us, and that Jesus offers his way to all who seek to live in harmony with God. Jesus has challenged Darrin to trust God, and to put his trust to the test in everyday life. And Darrin challenges his readers to walk with him on the road where, as Dorothy Day said, our lives will demonstrate the way we really think. In Jesus' words, his followers will be known not by their words but by their fruits (Matt 7:20).

This type of theology differs from academic theology. In these chapters we encounter not only a formidable, disciplined intellect but also heartfelt passion and moral courage. We see Darrin's different facets as he wrestles with classical issues (e.g., what does it mean that Christ assumed our nature?) and with his own life questions (e.g., fear, death, innocent suffering). We also encounter a deeply ecumenical Christian spirit. Darrin came to faith among Catholics, and has found his home among Mennonites. In company with both he works out his deeply biblical and orthodox faith that invites us to walk with him on the pilgrimage of discipleship. For many years we have known Darrin as a friend, and we have found him to be the person who emerges in this book—an engaging, vulnerable, and sympathetic companion on the road.

Alan and Eleanor Kreider

Preface

How much of myself (and my stuff) must I give up to follow Jesus? How does belonging to a faith community shape being a Christian? How do I walk in faith with friends whose faith is unclear or uncertain? What gives Christians hope in the face of power politics? Can I be pro-life and decry war, too? How do I make peace amidst the wrongs of the world? If you wonder about such questions and identify with such concerns, this book might be for you.

It was New Year's Eve 1998, and I was approaching thirty years old. I was visiting my brother and sister-in-law in Virginia, on the heels of what would prove to be a second successive unsuccessful attempt at securing a tenure-track college teaching position. My sister-in-law was in the habit of asking, not what resolutions one would make for the New Year, but rather: What question do you want God to answer for you in the coming year? My question that year was clear: *What is the meaning of discipleship? What does it cost to follow Jesus?*

At that point, I had already been pondering this question for more than a year. Now it seemed that my life was nearing a crossroads, a crisis point, a time of decision. I needed to know which way to commit my life—and what that way would cost me. At some point in the conversation, my brother went to retrieve a copy of Dietrich Bonhoeffer's *Cost of Discipleship* from his bookshelf and passed it on to me. As soon as I returned home, I began reading that book and came upon this answer: when Jesus calls someone, he bids him to come and die! I continued reading other books on Christian discipleship, including those from the Bruderhof community—*Salt and Light* by Eberhard Arnold and *Discipleship* by J. Heinrich Arnold. During the next year, and for years thereafter, God would continue to answer my question, time and again. And in response to God's answers,

Preface

I would undergo a dramatic conversion of personal life and a substantial shift of professional focus—I would "die" and begin a new life as a follower of Jesus.

From early on in this time of hearing and discerning my calling as a disciple, Psalm 143, the epigraph of this book, became my prayer: "Show me the road that I must walk." With this prayer as my path, I was led by the Holy Spirit "on level ground" to deliberately make sacrificial choices and spiritual commitments that continue to shape my life as a disciple. First and foremost, I withdrew from the pursuit of personal security and professional success in the academy, instead committing myself to use my gifts for the sake of the church by teaching wherever God would provide the opportunity and whatever needed to be taught. While this meant foregoing prospects for permanent employment and professional advancement, it has opened up possibilities for me to engage directly in the mission of the church through both urban service and international teaching. Simply making this commitment and seeking these opportunities did not settle all doubts or answer all questions, of course. Indeed, at several junctures over the intervening years I have had to carefully discern "the road that I must walk" even while prayerfully wondering/worrying whether I might have taken a wrong turn. Yet through each stage of the journey God has been faithful, providing meaningful teaching opportunities in both colleges and congregations, and life has been joyful, filled with friendships and communities of faith, hope, and love. I can thus testify that the promise of Jesus is trustworthy: those who have left homes or families or jobs for the sake of the kingdom of God will receive, not only life abundant when the kingdom comes, but also "very much more" than they had left behind "in this age" (Luke 19:28–30).

This is not a book *about* Christian discipleship, an attempt to define and describe it, but a book *by* a Christian disciple, the words of one who has sought to walk in the way of Jesus. This book represents my own wrestling with the call and cost of discipleship across my first decade as an intentional follower of Jesus. Arising from various circumstances and responding to various concerns, the several pieces collected here comprise a travelogue—or, better, a sketchbook—drawn from my journey of following Jesus. The chapters here are not academic essays or scholarly arguments, but personal reflections, scriptural meditations, and spiritual ponderings. Many tell stories, others issue challenges. Most are prose, some poetic. My prayer is that they may edify and encourage fellow pilgrims on the way.

Preface

The thirteen pieces I've selected reveal two sides of a single journey. Several are the personal reflections of "a disciple on the way." They relate and reflect on stories of my own frail (and sometimes failed) attempts at following Jesus, formative experiences through which I have learned the habits of discipleship. Others are a disciple's scriptural meditations and spiritual ponderings on "the way" of Jesus. They address concerns and conundrums that have vexed and perplexed my own heart and mind as a disciple, as well as explore the practical implications of the gospel for the disciples of Jesus. I have interspersed the personal reflections, scriptural meditations, and spiritual ponderings, prefacing each piece with a brief introduction that places it within my journey of following Jesus. Taken together, they disclose the discipleship of the heart intricately intertwined with the discipline of the mind. The book begins with a prayer reminding the disciple that following Jesus depends on God's grace. It concludes with a theological autobiography, an account of my pilgrimage to the gospel of peace in a time of war.

I've arranged the several pieces in four parts, each of which relates to a particular aspect of following Jesus and corresponds (more or less) with one of the Gospels. Part One is "The Call to Follow." Jesus' call to follow greets us in unexpected places and makes radical demands on our lives. The first chapter in this part reflects on a personal encounter that confronted me with my own call to follow and the question of the cost of discipleship. The second considers that crucial test for Christian disciples—Jesus' command that our love be perfect, including even our enemies—and reflects on my struggle to practice this perfect love in a difficult relationship. And the third reflects on Peter in the Gospel of Mark as he wrestles with what it means to confess Jesus as the Messiah and what it takes to follow this Messiah on the way to the cross.

Part Two is "The Valley of Shadows." Jesus' call to follow comes to us in a real world in which we are subject to fear and vulnerable to suffering. Following Jesus leads us through suffering and sorrow, but Jesus himself is God-with-us, God's promised presence to share our sorrows and walk with us through the vale of tears. The first chapter in this part recounts my own wandering in the shadows of fear and doubt—and God's sign of grace that showed me the way of faith and hope. The second recounts my experience walking in faith with a friend who was himself journeying through "the valley of the shadow of death." And the third reflects on the life, death, and resurrection of Jesus as God's personal response to the perennial question of innocent suffering.

Part Three is "The Way of Life." Jesus' call to follow comes to us in a fallen world hell-bent on destruction and death. Jesus promises his followers resurrection and life and calls us to bear witness to this good news in a dying world. The first chapter in this part reflects on the grace of Christ as integral to the way of life and my experience of the life of grace in intentional Christian community. The second summons the church to a consistent witness for life that reflects the gospel of God's life-giving love in Jesus and responds with life-affirming alternatives to the world's way of death. And the third draws out the political implications of confessing faith in Jesus as the One who is "the resurrection and the life" by reflecting on the life and death of Jesus in the Gospel of John.

Part Four is "The Way of Peace." Jesus' call to follow comes to us in a world gone wrong and warped by war. Jesus gives his followers peace and calls us to seek peace and make peace—to build communities of justice in a world of wrong, to seek the kingdom of God in a world at war, and to practice reconciliation in a world of division. The first chapter in this part recalls my own small part in practicing the way of peace during a time of war. The second reflects on the ecumenical efforts of Mennonites and Catholics to "maintain the unity of the Spirit in the bond of peace" (Eph 4:3) And the third recounts my journey of reconciliation to a city that had once been my country's enemy.

The reader will observe that the first chapter of Part One and the last chapter of Part Four both relate to and reflect on my earliest days of following Jesus. This bracketing of the book is deliberate. It serves to remind me that, as a follower of Jesus, I am a perpetual beginner.

This book is, in many ways, a token of gratitude to the various friends and communities that have shaped me and shared in my journey of discipleship. Accordingly, before submitting this book for publication, I invited several persons to read and reflect on these pages in order to help me discern the Spirit in this book. My thanks to: Duane and Lois Beck, Arthur Boers, Brenda Herb, Ivan Kauffman, Alan and Eleanor Kreider, Jay Landry, Abraham Newsom O.S.B., Paula Snyder Belousek, Janice Yordy Sutter, and Biff Weidman. Special thanks to Arthur Boers and to Alan and Eleanor Kreider for their counsel and encouragement in support of my work as a writer. I am humbled and honored that this book is graced by Alan and Ellie's foreword. Thanks, further, to Wipf & Stock and to my editor, Rodney

Preface

Clapp, for bringing this project to fruition. Finally, my best thanks to Paula Snyder Belousek, who has been my faithful companion on the journey.

All this is from God,
and all by grace.

(2 Cor 5:17–20; 1 Cor 15:10)

Darrin W. Snyder Belousek
Lima, Ohio
January 2014

Prologue

Plea for Grace—
A Disciple's Prayer

Grant in me, O Lord, a generous heart,
that I might do justice
by sharing with those in need
the bread you give me day by day.

Grant in me, O Lord, a merciful heart,
that I might love kindness
by forgiving others their debts
as you have forgiven mine.

Grant in me, O Lord, a pure heart,
that I might walk humbly with God
by seeking the righteousness of God's kingdom
above all earthly power and treasure.

The Call to Follow

*[Jesus] said to him, "Follow me."
And he got up and followed him.*

—Mark 2:14

*"If any want to become my followers,
let them deny themselves and take up their cross
and follow me."*

—Mark 8:34

1

Not I, but Christ—
A Disciple's Call

*I have been crucified with Christ;
and it is no longer I who live,
but Christ who lives in me.*

—GALATIANS 2:19–20

This is my first written reflection on the Christian life, dating from 1999–2000. The occasion was an invitation from the pastors of my congregation, who asked members to share their experiences relating to people on the margins. I took this as an opportunity to reflect on a series of such relationships, and one in particular, that had forced me to think about what it means to be a Christian—that, indeed, had confronted me with the question of whether I would commit myself to following Jesus. The first of these relationships, recounted below, took place during the spring of 1997 in Cambridge, England, where I spent a term researching and writing my dissertation for my doctoral studies at the University of Notre Dame. It is that encounter that set my heart and mind in motion.

The other visitors would come after my return to South Bend, Indiana, where over a period of a year, 1998–1999, God sent several men in succession to my front door (literally!). Each one presented his story of trouble (which I did not know whether to believe) and returned several times with requests for

The Call to Follow

help. As each kept appearing, the convicting words of the late Keith Green, from his song "Asleep in the Light," kept coming to mind:

> He brings people to your door / and you turn them away / as you smile and say, / "God bless you, be at peace" / and all heaven just weeps / Jesus came to your door / you've left him out on the street.[1]

Each time, then, I would greet my visitor, invite him in, and listen to his request. Responding to these requests, which usually came at night (and some of which I did refuse), took me to places and placed me in situations I had never been in before. Later I would wrestle with God in prayer: What do you want from me? At last I concluded: God is asking me to do what I had hesitated to do in Cambridge—to sacrifice everything. These situations were presenting me with a test of faith: Do I trust God enough to give away my money? To risk my safety to help another? To become entangled with a stranger's life?

During that year I often felt overwhelmed by the demands of these situations. I even found myself pleading with God that I had reached the limits of my patience and endurance and that he should "remove the cup" from me. God answered my prayer, not by removing the cup but by assuring me that "my grace is sufficient for you" (2 Cor 12:9). And so, three times during that year, I gave away all the money I had, leaving myself only enough to pay rent and buy food for that month. I did so, not because I thought my generosity would save those men (only God knew what they really needed), but rather because I realized that doing so, as an act of trust in God, was necessary for me to "work out [my] own salvation with fear and trembling" in response to the work of God's grace in me (Phil 2:12–13).

It was these tokens of sacrifice that opened my heart to desire that I make my whole life an offering to God. After all, as Keith Green put it so effectively in his song "To Obey Is Better Than Sacrifice," God does not need my money, he wants my life! And it was God's grace in sustaining me by the Holy Spirit through the emotional and financial challenges of that year that enabled me to trust God so that I might make the crucial decisions, both personal and professional, that diverted my life down a different path.

∼

---

1. Keith Green, "Asleep in the Light" (1978).

Not I, but Christ—A Disciple's Call

What Is My Duty?

> "I confess to Almighty God,
> and to you, my brothers and sisters,
> that I have sinned through my own fault
> in my thoughts and in my words,
> by what I have done and what I have failed to do . . ."[2]

Think for a moment about the parable of the Good Samaritan (Luke 10:25–37). Do the priest and the Levite, who both "passed by on the other side of the road" (Luke 10:31–32), actually sin in what they fail to do, by not helping the man who "fell into the hands of robbers"? Jesus clearly implies that they do sin—each neglects his neighbor and thus fails to fulfill the law of love.

Which raises the question: Which of the actions that I don't do are sins, failures to do what is required of me? Where is the line between duty and choice? The all-too-human way to draw this line begins with the ego-self—the *I*. And this *I* tends to draw the line according to self-interest.

That is precisely how the lawyer in the parable wants to define his duty under the law. Jesus tells the parable, you will remember, in reply to a lawyer who has asked, "What must I do to inherit eternal life?" Jesus asks him to interpret the Torah on this question; and the lawyer recites what Jesus elsewhere acknowledges to be the two chief covenant commandments that summarize the law and the prophets—love God, love your neighbor (Luke 10:25–27; cf. Mark 12:28–34; Matt 22:34–40). Jesus replies approvingly, "You have given the right answer; do this, and you will live" (Luke 10:28). But the lawyer, "wanting to justify himself," asks Jesus: "And who is my neighbor?" (Luke 10:29). The lawyer here seeks to qualify what is required of him, to limit his duty by circumscribing the category of persons ("neighbor") whom the Torah commands him to love. He wants a rational calculation to determine in advance how far the covenant obligation to "love your neighbor as yourself" extends. Implicitly, the pivot-point of the lawyer's question is not the neighbor but *I*.

Christian discipleship, however, begins with *not I*: Jesus said, "If any want to become my followers, let them deny themselves and take up their cross and follow me. For those who want to save their life will lose it, and those who lose their life for my sake, and for the sake of the gospel, will save it" (Mark 8:34–35). If I am to follow Jesus, *I* must first in some sense *die*; in

---

2. Prayer of confession from the Roman Rite of the Catholic Church.

losing my self—by death of the rational, autonomous, self-interested ego—I will truly live. For, Paul says, by taking up my cross, following Jesus and being crucified with him, Christ will live in me: "I am crucified with Christ, nevertheless I live; yet not I, but Christ liveth in me" (Gal 2:19–20 KJV). But then, if it is not *I* who draws the line between duty and choice, what then is required of me? And who decides?

The Disciple's Call: Be Attentive

The prophet of the Lord instructs us: "He has told you, O mortal, what is good; and what does the Lord require of you but to do justice, and to love kindness, and to walk humbly with your God?" (Mic 6:8). In order to act with justice, mercy, and humility on behalf of those who are poor, oppressed, or outcast, I must already be aware of injustice, deprivation, and exclusion where it exists. And I will not become aware of injustice unless I make myself aware of those who suffer injustice, deprivation, or exclusion—that is, I must refocus attention, away from the self-interested *I* to the margins, to persons who have been overlooked. To fulfill what is required of me, to obey my Lord's call to discipleship, I must begin by *being attentive*—attentive to the word of the Lord, attentive to the cry of the poor. Thus, the first sin of omission—often hidden beneath the justifications and rationalizations that pave the road for sins of commission—is the failure to pay attention. My first responsibility is *to hear, to look, to take notice*. In this way, I might imitate the God of our Lord Jesus Christ, who, faithful to his word and his people, attends to the plight of the poor and oppressed:

> After a long time the king of Egypt died. The Israelites groaned under their slavery, and cried out. Out of the slavery their cry for help rose up to God. God *heard* their groaning, and God *remembered* his covenant with Abraham, Isaac, and Jacob. God *looked* upon the Israelites, and God *took notice* of them. (Exod 2:23–25)

This call to be attentive first caught my attention some years ago while reading Albert Camus' collection of stories, *Exile and the Kingdom*. The following poem then came to me:

> Who are these silent ones that rage without sound?
> Has helplessness and despair numbed their tongues?
> Or has the assiduous march of life drummed out of them the will to speak?

Who will listen to their cry in the restless night?
For who could hear let alone understand the desperately quieted
voice of the dispossessed?
But their silence is our sentence,
and their future is our fate.
If we attend not to their unsung song,
if we heed not their inaudible warning,
if we do not listen to the silence of the voiceless,
from our hands will drip their blood
and upon our heads will fall their avenging.

In our shadow rests our responsibility,
at our margins lies our meaning.
What is needed to avert our attention?

The call to be attentive finds keen expression in the work and writing of two women who gave their lives to others in suffering. Simone Weil emphasized that true, empathic love of neighbor essentially requires being consciously attentive to the suffering other as another like oneself:

> The love of our neighbor in all its fullness . . . is a recognition that the sufferer exists, not only as a unit in a collection, or a specimen of the social category labeled "unfortunate," but as a man, exactly like us, who was one day stamped with a special mark of affliction.[3]

And Mother Theresa taught us that we must not only succor the suffering, but first and foremost we must respond to the need for dignity, respect, and welcome of those who suffer by recognizing them as "Christ in distressing disguise."

Attending to the Margins

Many injustices require our attention in this world. One of the difficulties that stand in the way of addressing the persistent problem of homelessness in our society is that homeless persons themselves are often not only homeless, but also voiceless, nameless, and faceless to those of us in privileged positions who possess the power to pass them by without taking notice. And so they will remain unnoticed on the margins of our lives until we, in servant spirit, deliberately avert attention from ourselves, regard their divinely-imaged humanity with the eyes of a conscience convicted—and,

---

3. Weil, *Waiting for God*, 115.

rather than speaking about or even for them, let their own voices resound with resolute clarity in our ears and hearts.

In order to be attentive to suffering others, such as those who are homeless, we must encounter them in their own world; and this requires that we be displaced from those comfortable spaces in which we are at home. Where we feel at home, the familiarity of the space frees us from having to take notice of our surroundings in order to orient our activity; it is precisely our ability to *not* attend to distraction that frees us to function purposefully and efficiently. Along the avenues and pavements of our cities, homeless persons can become distractions that familiarity enables us to ignore such that they pass through our view unnoticed. It is thus when we are in some way displaced from our familiar space into an alien place that we begin to pay attention, that we must of necessity take notice.

The very lives of Simone Weil and Mother Theresa teach us this lesson by example. Weil displaced herself from houses of comfort and halls of privilege to the factories of the laborers and fields of the peasants. Mother Theresa displaced herself from the safety of the cloister in Albania to the suffering of the streets in Calcutta. My own all-too-human tendency, after coming into contact with a suffering person, is to want to wash off the suffering, to purify myself of suffering by separating from the sufferer, to distance myself from him so as to convince myself that his suffering is not mine—and, hence, that I am not responsible for him.

Henri Nouwen taught us by his life that, once we learn to recognize Christ in the suffering presence of the other, a truly compassionate response in the face of the other leads one to dwell in the midst of the other's suffering:

> Here we see what compassion means. It is not a bending toward the underprivileged from a privileged position . . . On the contrary, compassion means going directly to those people and places where suffering is most acute and building a home there.[4]

Dwelling amidst the suffering of others requires that we resolutely plant ourselves in the soil where suffering grows, outside the walls of pretended purity that hide suffering others from our view and that hide us from our responsibility—we must get dirty. Thomas Merton, while discerning his own vocation before entering Gethsemani Abbey, was convicted of the potential even for the religiously devoted to retreat behind the safety of

---

4. Nouwen et al., *Compassion*, 27.

monastery walls and remain ignorant of suffering and one's responsibility for it.

> Instead of seeing Christ suffering in His members, and instead of going to help Him, Who said: "Whatsoever you did to the least of these my brethren, you did it to Me," we preferred our own comfort: we averted our eyes from such a spectacle, because it made us feel uneasy: the thought of so much dirt nauseated us—and we never stopped to think that we, perhaps, might be partly responsible for it.[5]

A Disciple's Margin Call

My own displacement from the familiar occurred in the spring of 1997, when I studied for a semester at the University of Cambridge in England. Nearly every day, on my usual way home from the university, I encountered a homeless man, who sat with two dogs in a storefront, almost always the same one, asking passersby for spare change. Until then, my only real encounter with homeless persons had been as a volunteer at the South Bend Center for the Homeless. At the Center, my interaction with homeless persons was neatly controlled by the institutional structure, and my responsibility to the guests was not only narrowly circumscribed by my role as a children's tutor, but was always left behind when I left the building. Moreover, the more familiar I became with the geography of the center, the freer I felt to ignore those guests who did not concern me. How I should respond to this man now before me on the edge of the pavement, outside the security and predictability of the walls at the Center, I didn't know.

Though he was a friendly and gentle man, always thanking me kindly for whatever spare change I gave him and even thanking me when I said I had nothing to give, this was an uncontrolled situation. Instinctively, I sought to control it by keeping the relationship on my own terms and thereby keeping him on the periphery of my concern, so as to limit my sense of responsibility toward him. I didn't have courage enough to stop and ask him, "What are you going through?"—much less to listen to him speak in his own voice. I did not invite him into my home, much less attempt to dwell in the midst of his suffering. I did not even ask him his name, nor as much as prayed for him. The possibility of such familiarity and intimacy—the

---

5. Merton, *Seven Storey Mountain*, 341.

The Call to Follow

thought of close contact with his uncleanness—frightened me. The more I knew of his situation, the more vulnerable to the world of his suffering I might become and the more responsible for his situation I might feel.

I noticed the suffering—or, rather, I noticed my own discomfort in the face of his suffering—but I failed to recognize and respond to the human dignity of the sufferer himself. Each morning and after meeting him each evening, I passed by a church displaying a sign, upon which was written:

> Come to me, all you that are weary and are carrying heavy burdens, and I will give you rest. Take my yoke upon you, and learn from me; for I am gentle and humble in heart, and you will find rest for your souls. For my yoke is easy, and my burden is light. (Matt 11:28–30)

Though I read and pondered the meaning of this message for myself, not once did I recognize in these words the face of the suffering man on the edge of the pavement—and so, too, did I fail to recognize in him the incarnate face of the very One whose words these are.

Instead, I preoccupied myself with the philosophical-moral question, What do I owe him? How much money should I give him each time I pass by? Only the loose change in my pocket? This posed a dilemma. In British currency, there is a gold £1 coin, rather than a paper note, in addition to silver coins of lesser value. To give him all the change in my pocket, then, would sometimes be to give away a few pounds (and, with the exchange rate, several dollars), not just a few pence. That seemed too much to require. So, each day as I anticipated passing his usual place on the edge of the pavement, I would hurriedly thrust my hand into my pocket to feel what coins I had and to sort them by touch. I did this to save myself the embarrassment of pulling out a handful of change in front of him and having him see me sort out the silver for him and keep back the gold for myself. A few times, though, not paying attention to where I was, I found myself standing before him fumbling nervously with my change; and if on these occasions I gave him gold as well as silver, it was only because I feared his resentment. Conscious of my sin, I rationalized with myself to appease my conscience: If I owed him all the change in my pocket, then what about the £5, £10, or £20-pound note in my wallet? And if I owed him all that was in my wallet, what about the £250 in my checking account? Would I owe him all that, too? Didn't reason (my self-interested *I* said) demand a limit somewhere? So, I settled for the minimum, and continued to give him only the silver coins from my pocket.

I sought to fulfill my responsibility, but I missed the point of the prophet's teaching—mercy and humility are to qualify justice. I sought to do justice, but conceived of it as only a monetary exchange between interested parties, a transaction to be defined and calculated by the ideal rational agent. And so, like the Pharisees and scribes, I "neglected the weightier matters of the law: justice and mercy and faith" (Matt 23:23). I was straining gnats only to swallow camels! I had presumed that I could circumscribe the sphere of my responsibility toward him as I saw fit, that I could draw a line between myself and him and say, "This far will I go and no further, and that is far enough." I presumed that I could calculate for myself how much I owed him, that I could fix in advance the cost of discipleship. But, again, had I not missed the point? Before the call to discipleship costs me a dollar, it first requires me to *give attention*: the other in whose suffering presence I stand summons me to compassion and mercy. In all my self-interested calculating, rationalizing, and justifying, *I* had eclipsed *him* from view—and therefore Christ, too.

Let's return to the parable of the Good Samaritan. The lawyer's self-justifying definition of the covenant via legal casuistry is embodied in the parable by the priest and the Levite, who both "passed by on the other side" of the road (Luke 10:31–32). "But a Samaritan while traveling came near him; and when he saw him, he was moved with pity. He went to him . . ." (Luke 10:33–34). What differentiates the Samaritan from the priest and the Levite? Both the priest and Levite also "saw him." The crucial difference between the Samaritan's show of mercy and the priest's and Levite's shows of indifference occurs before this. While the priest was merely "going down that road," and the Levite only "came to the place," the Samaritan "came near him" (Luke 10:31–33). This "coming near *him*"—in contrast with just "going down *the road*" or "coming to *the place*"—is the crucial difference. We could say that, while all three passersby *saw* the man, only the Samaritan *took notice* of him. Or, we might say that while the priest and the Levite bypass only a specific instance of the general category "unfortunate" (which can be regarded with indifference), the Samaritan encounters *this* man like himself in *his* suffering.

The Samaritan's steps are redirected toward the man ("he went to him") only because his *attention* had already been redirected—from his travel plans and future purposes to this man, here, now. What drew the Samaritan *near him*, toward this man lying beaten beside the road? The man's cry for mercy, we may imagine. We could even imagine that the Samaritan's merciful response imitates God's merciful response to the Israelites' cry for help out of slavery and oppression: He *heard* his groaning by the side of the road, *remembered* the covenant ("love your neighbor as yourself"), *looked* upon the man, and *took notice* of him. As God "took notice" of the Israelites in their suffering and then "came down to deliver them" (Exod 3:7–8), the Samaritan inclined his ear, opened his heart, and then "came near" to deliver this man from his suffering at the edge of the road.

Before dispensing his material provisions and pledging his financial means to assist the man (Luke 10:34–35), the Samaritan committed first his *attention* and then his whole self to the man in his suffering—he surrendered his *I* to the other's plea for compassion and mercy. The Samaritan's self-displacement to the "other side" of the road and into the world of that one man's suffering—this movement of compassion and mercy in the suffering presence of the other, this *giving attention* to the other prior to ever asking "Is he my neighbor?" or "How much do I owe him?"—fulfills the life-promising covenant (Luke 10:25–28, 37). Jesus' call to discipleship, disclosed by the suffering presence of the other, is thus beyond—indeed, before—any and all calculation of enlightened self-interest by the ideal rational agent.

Now back to the edge of the pavement in Cambridge: Though a man's body burdened by hunger be bowed over, though his eyes filled with the shame of homelessness be cast down, though his voice drowned by the despair of powerlessness be quieted, his outstretched arm and upturned, opened hand reveals the destitution of his situation and summons a compassionate, merciful response. The opened hand of the hungry stranger is the hand of Jesus, inviting me to fellowship at God's banquet table of grace. Before me, then, manifest in the flesh, was Christ in "distressing disguise" (Matt 25:31–46). Here, in the embodied, suffering presence of this one man created in God's holy image was my call to discipleship. The only way to elude my responsibility would have been to avert my eyes and ears, close my heart, and cross to the far side of the pavement. But I could indifferently sidestep him and my responsibility no more than he could simply get up and walk away from his homelessness.

Discipleship begins with Christ, not *I*—"not I, but Christ." In the suffering presence of the other, I am faced with the Christ who summons me to responsibility: to do justice, love mercy, and walk humbly with God—and first, to be attentive, listen, remember, look, take notice.

A few years later I was able to draw a lesson from my encounters with the man on the edge of the pavement in Cambridge. While serving as a church mission worker in South Bend, Indiana, I took an assignment at the Advocacy Center. Operated and supported by the churches of the county, this faith-based ministry served people in crisis situations by dispensing both material and financial assistance as well as advocating on their behalf with various public service agencies. We dispensed everything from toiletries to socks to school supplies to bus tokens to gas vouchers to food vouchers to utility payments to rental deposits to agency referrals to personal advice. A place of last resort, we served thousands of clients each year. My primary responsibility was to do intake interviews with the clients and then discern with the director how best to offer assistance, referral, or advocacy. In doing so, we sought to serve our clients' individual needs and not box them into various social categories of "unfortunates." As I served the clients and observed my fellow volunteers during those three years, I came to see that the most important thing we did, what characterized us as a Christian ministry rather than a mere social agency, was serving hot coffee and listening to people tell their stories—satisfying the very human need for welcome, respect, and dignity. I thus realized that the proper question with which to begin the intake interview was not "What do you need?" or "How may we help you?" but rather "What is your situation? What are you going through?"

2

What Would You Do?
A Disciple's Test(imony)

> "You have heard that it was said,
> 'An eye for an eye and a tooth for a tooth.'
> But I say to you, Do not resist an evildoer. . . .
> You have heard that it was said,
> 'You shall love your neighbor and hate your enemy.'
> But I say to you, Love your enemies
> and pray for those who persecute you,
> so that you may be children of your Father in heaven . . .
> Be perfect, therefore, as your heavenly Father is perfect."
>
> —Matthew 5:38–45, 48

> We must, then, prepare our hearts and bodies
> for the battle of holy obedience to his instructions.
> What is not possible to us by nature,
> let us ask the Lord to supply by the help of his grace.
>
> —Rule of Saint Benedict[1]

---

1. Fry, *Rule of St. Benedict 1980*, 165.

The Call to Follow

A year after committing my whole life to following Jesus, I was presented with an opportunity to put that commitment into practice through voluntary service. I accepted a mission assignment in an inner-city neighborhood, which introduced me to the realities of both urban ministry and intentional Christian community (more on the latter in "What We Live By," below). Not long after undertaking this assignment and taking residence in the neighborhood, God sent yet another visitor to my door—someone who would strain my trust and stretch my patience far more severely than had any of my previous visitors from God. This relationship not only put my commitment to follow Jesus to the test but also taught me the difficult truth that not all that is broken in this world can be put right through good intentions and kind actions: there remains a residue of resistance to grace that can be overcome and healed only by God. I have reflected on this experience from the angle of the perennial question "What would you do?" so that I might add my testimony to the cloud of witnesses who have testified with their lives that following Jesus means practicing the perfect love of God that Jesus demonstrated at the cross for us—love even for one's enemy.

~

The Test of Discipleship

What would you do if a stranger invaded your home? If a gunman was on the loose in your neighborhood and threatening children? A band of soldiers forced their way into your faith community's place of prayer to arrest your beloved pastor? Would you draw and use a weapon against the enemy?

This is the standard type of question put to those who commit themselves to loving enemies on account of Christian discipleship. The gospel calls us to follow Jesus in the way of the cross and pursue God's way of peacemaking, trusting for deliverance in God's life-restoring promise of resurrection rather than in the life-destroying power of weapons. Making sense of such a faith commitment requires that Christian disciples give a serious answer to this standard question; for dealing with enemies is the crucial test of following Jesus.

As typically asked, however, "What if" is a loaded question that itself begs for careful analysis. It makes many questionable assumptions and

What Would You Do? A Disciple's Test(imony)

typically prefigures the dilemma "kill or be killed" before any dialogue on the question can take place. For such an analysis, one would do well to consult John Howard Yoder's book titled after this question.[2] Here I will make the observation that the question can be asked of the disciple in either of two ways. The "What if" question could be a test of consistency of Christian discipleship: "If you would defend your family with force, then isn't your answer to the war question wrong?" Insofar as Christian discipleship makes no claim to be an airtight ethical system of absolute rules, the question in this sense is somewhat off the mark though still important to consider.[3] The "What if" question might also be a way of getting at one's duty to defend the innocent: "I can accept that you won't defend your own life, but don't you have a responsibility to protect the lives of others?" The question in this sense is right on the mark: Yes, every Christian has a duty to take personal risks in order to do justice for the vulnerable and weak; discipleship cannot be used as an escape from responsibility (i.e., "nothing" is an inadequate answer to the "What if" question). So, I will take up the question in this second sense.

I don't think there is any one answer to this question, a general formula to handle all cases. There are many possible Christ-like ways to respond to and resist evil in a given situation, of which the Yoder book gives several examples by way of personal testimonies. Moreover, just as with violent responses to evil, there is no guarantee that nonviolent responses to evil will be successful in the sense of resulting in an outcome that avoids harm to all persons involved (or even harm to the innocent). Christian discipleship is not a pragmatic method for generating preferred outcomes but rather is the habitual posture or characteristic disposition by which the disciple approaches the world. And that posture is essentially one of vulnerability and humility, of dependence upon and trust in God's providence and power for deliverance and vindication rather than one's own intentions and abilities.[4] Christian discipleship takes on the cruciform posture of God's incarnation (cf. Phil 2:5–8): the posture of Jesus in the garden of agony yielding himself to divine purpose; the posture of Jesus being handed over to the arresting soldiers and led off by force; the posture of Jesus being accused, beaten and mocked in the courts of power; the posture of Jesus being crucified—all

---

2. Yoder, *What Would You Do?*
3. See ibid. and Roth, *Choosing Against War*.
4. Concerning the cruciform posture of Christian discipleship, see Jones, *Dismissing Jesus*.

the while forgiving his enemies (Luke 23:34) and "entrusting himself to the one who judges justly" (1 Pet 2:21–23). Not only is a cruciform posture incompatible with wielding one's weapon against the enemy; but, having become habituated to this posture, even having a weapon to hand in the first place is inconceivable. A cruciform posture in our world may not work in every instance to defeat evil (again, violent force does not always work either and sometimes provokes more violence), but the chief point is to remain faithful to God's way revealed in Jesus.[5]

The Testimony of a Disciple

For sure, Christian discipleship in the face of evil that holds out love for the enemy does not come naturally to me—I know too well how many lives I've murdered in my heart, if not with my hands (cf. Matt 5:21–22). Thus, for me, Christian discipleship must be a spiritual discipline, a practice of daily conversion rooted in prayer ("Lord, make me an instrument of your peace") and deep trust in God's grace ("Into your hands, I commit my spirit"). Christian discipleship requires that I "put on the whole armor of God" so that I may stand by God's power against the evil of the day (Eph 6).

Christian discipleship also requires active imagination, thinking outside the box of predictable possibilities—kill or be killed—that the "What if" question creates. During the summer of 2001 I led a Sunday school class in a study of the Yoder book. By studying the personal stories related in the several essays, I was prompted to imagine myself into the real-life situations being described and ask myself: How might I respond in a Christ-like way if I were in such a situation? How might my actions conform to the cross in a situation with potential for violence? Reflecting upon the example of Jesus—who by his intercessory peacemaking effectively put his own body between our violence and the cross, interrupting the cycle of violence and vengeance by absorbing enmity and returning mercy—I imagined that the very least I could do would be to put myself in the middle, risking my own body and life for the sake of the person under attack/threat.[6] A few months

---

5. For real-world examples of actual Christian communities living out this cruciform posture as a shared commitment, see Coble, *Cotton Patch for the Kingdom* and Mosley, *With Our Own Eyes*.

6. Cf. Yoder, *What Would You Do?*, 26: "the congruent application of meaningful sacrifice would be for me to intervene in such a way that, without my destroying the aggressor, would refocus his attack upon me instead of upon the originally intended victim."

What Would You Do? A Disciple's Test(imony)

later I was given an opportunity to put to the test what I had already prayerfully prepared in my mind and heart to do.

In the summer of 2000 I had met a middle-aged woman, whose name I'll abbreviate S., who came by my inner-city house one day looking for some work to do. As I was to learn, she suffered from paranoid schizophrenia but when on medication was capable of relatively decent social relations, though she did not always choose such behavior. When off her medication she could be either incoherent or highly volatile, and in such situations it was very difficult to deal with her rationally because one never knew which edge of reality she might be on and what comment or action would push her over the edge. Although she received government welfare and disability checks, she was not capable of managing her situation well enough to avoid being homeless and, though vulnerable to exploitation by those who wanted her check money, she refused the kind of accountability necessary for others to help her into a stable living situation. To make her transient situation work, she often engaged shamelessly in various forms of deception, fraud, manipulation, and moral blackmail (accusations of racism or "pity me" comments) to get what she wanted even from those who were willing to help her, including me. She even attempted to steal my wallet on one occasion and, I suspect, once stole our petty cash from the voluntary service unit.

For a year or so as we became better acquainted I paid S. to do odd jobs around the yard from time to time, sometimes gave her lunch, and did occasionally hand out money after hearing dubious stories of need that supposedly required immediate attention. Sometimes the immediate need was very real, and I made several trips with her to the psychiatric hospital when she had bottomed out without her medication and one trip to the emergency room for a serious hand wound (whether the result of an assault or self-inflicted, I didn't know). During this year, I spent much time in prayer regarding how to deal with this evolving situation. I often struggled with the question of whether I had helped her enough or had done the right thing and wondered what it meant to love her and where grace might be found in this relationship. Many times S. would show up in the middle of the night—2:00 or 3:00 A.M.—pounding on my door or rattling my window until I would rouse from bed to see what she wanted. At times, at my wit's end and feeling stretched beyond my patience and means, I could utter only the prayer: "Lord, help S., help me, help me to help S." In my praying I did come to hold fast to one thing: despite knowing that she

The Call to Follow

was at times deliberately deceiving me and even using others to manipulate me, and despite feeling quite angry about this, I resolved not to deal with her according to her actions. This renunciation of retaliation—not giving payback or repaying evil for evil to those who harm us—is, I take it, the heart of what Jesus meant when he taught us to not forcibly resist evildoers: "But if anyone strikes you on the right cheek, turn the other also; and if anyone wants to sue you and take your coat, give your cloak as well; and if anyone forces you to go one mile, go also the second mile" (Matt 5:39–41).

In the fall of 2001 S. began to talk of making me her payee so that I would receive her government checks and be responsible for seeing to it that she got what she needed. I welcomed this suggestion. Her past payees (including her own daughter) had used and abused her as much or more as she had abused others, so I saw it as a way of breaking that cycle. I also saw it as a way of getting some leverage on her situation so as to be able to demand a certain level of accountability on her part. Almost immediately after she officially made me her payee in the spring of 2002, the manipulation and deception kicked into high gear. Although I was suspicious, I didn't fully catch on to her scheme until she had extracted her total month's benefit from me, before I even received her first check. A week later, when her checks were to arrive in the mail, the whole situation reached the boiling point. I never saw the checks in the mail. Evidently, she had conspired with someone else to have the checks stolen out of my mailbox before I could get them, which could then be forged at a check cashing place; then when I didn't receive them, the plan went, I could call the government office and report the checks missing and the government would issue new ones (apparently a common form of fraud). She was attempting a double-fraud, of both me and the government. She succeeded with only defrauding me—as soon as I figured out what she was doing I called the Social Security office, had my name removed as payee, and instructed them to not issue new checks.

I was at an end-point with her—that she could do this to me after all I had done for her! In the meantime, before I could have it out with her, the situation turned against an innocent bystander. The day the first check was to have arrived, S. (I found out later) had shown up to my house at around the time the mail was to be delivered. She hounded the mail carrier about her check, demanding that it be given directly to her and accusing the mail carrier of stealing it. She then came by the house later that day after I was home to see if the check had come; I told her I had not received

What Would You Do? A Disciple's Test(imony)

it and that she should come back the next day. I also reminded her that her entire check would belong to me because of all the money I had loaned her against her checks, at which she became enraged, accusing me of exploiting her and trying to steal her check.

Two days later, when the second check was to arrive, I was home for the mail delivery. S. showed up to ask about her check; I told her the mail had not yet come and invited her to wait on the porch. When the mail carrier came to the house she grew hostile toward him. There was no check in the mail (evidently due to a computer error, I learned later). She accused the mail carrier of stealing her check. After a barrage of angry words and vulgarity from S., I managed to get her to calm down and be quiet long enough to hear from the mail carrier the story from two days earlier. I then confronted S. by asking her what that was about. She refused to respond and instead went after the mail carrier. Before I knew what was happening, she had taken a brick from our porch and hurled it at him, barely missing. Without thinking much about what to do, I picked up the brick and put myself between S. and the mail carrier, who had backed away to a distance. I sternly told her to sit down and be quiet, which she did. I turned to talk with the mail carrier to get more of the story when she again became enraged and rushed at him, this time hurling threats to harm and even kill him, claiming she could get a gun and would shoot him. I stayed in the middle, telling S. to back off. She did back off, but instead of going back to the porch she went and grabbed a small tree branch that had fallen. Brandishing this as a weapon, she again rushed at him hurling threats.

Despite this escalation in her violence, I had no intention of trying to forcibly arrest her; nonetheless, I was determined not to let her get to the mail carrier. Not at all sure whether she would try to harm me, I kept myself in the middle and persisted in calling her name to redirect her attention from him to me. Eventually she did look at me, and when I had her attention I demanded she give me the stick and go and sit on the porch. Instead of handing over the branch, she threw it on the ground toward him, but then she did go and sit down. I picked up the branch and broke it in half, tossing the pieces far away from us.

At that point, the mail carrier took the opportunity to disengage and move on, telling her that he intended to report this incident (assaulting a mail carrier is a federal felony). As he proceeded to walk down the street to deliver mail at the next several houses, S. once more got up and started after him. I thought for a moment about what to do and decided I could not

The Call to Follow

just abandon the situation, so I followed after her and again put myself in between, instructing her several times to walk in the other direction. I had to keep this up halfway down the block until the mail carrier finished his deliveries on our street, got into his truck, and drove away. At that point, S. turned against me, hurling accusations and threats. She started back toward our house, threatening to take the brick and put it through our (new) picture window. Now I got on the other side, standing between her and the house, and asked her to leave. Eventually she did walk away, leaving me quite unsure whether she would return to follow through on her threat. Thankfully, she did not.

A week or so later S. came around again. At this point I confronted her with all her deceptions and manipulations, which she only denied. I then insisted that if she wanted anything more to do with me, she would have to sincerely apologize to the mail carrier. When she came around again a few weeks later, she told me that she had apologized (which the mail carrier had told me about in the meantime) and I thanked her for doing that. She offered to pay back what she owed me out of her future checks. I declined her offer and forgave her debt, something I had already resolved to do in payer: "And forgive us our debts, as we have forgiven our debtors" (Matt 6:12).

Looking back on these events, I'd like to be able to say that my other-cheek-turning, debtor-forgiving action proved radically transforming for S. and our relationship. It did not. This incident did bring things to a crisis point in her life: she was jailed pending prosecution for assaulting the mail carrier (partly on my own statement to a federal investigator). Instead of prison (which would have done her no good and perhaps even harm, something I emphasized in my statement), the judge prudently suspended sentence and ordered S. to be admitted to the state hospital, after which she stayed awhile with extended family in a downstate city. Months later she returned to South Bend looking healthy and I was glad to see her doing well. I would continue to see S. now and then around the neighborhood where I lived and at the Advocacy Center where I volunteered, but I did not trust her anymore and no longer welcomed her at our house (to avoid exposing my unwitting housemates to her antics). Eventually the signs of disorder began to appear again; the distorting forces of mental illness are indeed powerful. I don't know what happened to S. after that. But I continued to pray for her—and still do.

3

I Do Not Know this Man—
A Disciple's Confession

*Then after a little while the bystanders again said to Peter,
"Certainly you are one of them; for you are a Galilean."
But he began to curse, and he swore an oath,
"I do not know this man you are talking about."*
—Mark 14:71

*But the medium is Christ
whom no one can truly know
unless he follow him in his life,
and no one may follow him
unless he has first known him.*
— Hans Denck (1526)[1]

The occasion of this reflection was my study of the Gospel of Mark in Willard Swartley's class at Anabaptist Mennonite Biblical Seminary in Elkhart, Indiana. Mark's narrative of discipleship is marked by the contrast of Peter's

---

1. Quoted from Klaassen, *Anabaptism in Outline*, 87.

two declarations concerning Jesus—his confession of Jesus as the Messiah and his denial that he even knows Jesus. As is well known, Peter's confession is immediately followed by a rebuke from Jesus because Peter rejects Jesus' prophecy of his passion. What has been less noticed, if not overlooked, is that Peter's denial is immediately preceded by a series of actions that deny Jesus in deed before Peter denies him in word. It occurred to me that this series of actions, culminating in the denial, reveals Peter's own struggle with the call to follow Jesus. That insight led to another: Peter's struggle to follow Jesus all the way to the cross actually begins at his confession—Peter cannot follow Jesus to the cross precisely because he cannot confess a Messiah who is crucified. And this led to the inverse insight: Peter cannot confess a Messiah who is crucified because he is not yet ready to take up his own cross. The dialectical relationship between confessing Jesus and following Jesus was formulated by the early Anabaptist, Hans Denck: to know Christ is to follow him, and to follow Christ is to know him. I saw in all this a challenge both for myself as a disciple and for the church as a discipleship community: Is my decision to follow Jesus at the same time a willingness to take up my own cross? Is the church's confession of Jesus as Lord and Savior at the same time a pledge to stand in solidarity with those who bear crosses in our world?

I wrote the first draft of this reflection during a 2004 Lenten retreat at Saint Gregory's Abbey in Three Rivers, Michigan. A few paragraphs from this reflection were adapted with my permission for use in Swartley, Covenant of Peace.

∼

Who Is Jesus?

One usually thinks that Peter's confession of Jesus as Messiah comes following a discussion between Jesus and the disciples at the beginning of their journey on the way from Galilee to Jerusalem (Mark 8:27ff.).[2] Jesus questions the disciples, "Who do people say that I am?" According to the disciples, some folks think Jesus is John the Baptist, still others Elijah, and yet others "one of the prophets." More interested in his disciples' understanding of who he is than the varied and changing opinions of the crowds,

---

2. All citations of Scripture in this chapter are from the Gospel of Mark unless indicated otherwise.

Jesus asks them, "But who do you say that I am?" Peter answers quickly, as if for the rest, and as if he were certain of what he says: "You are the Messiah" (8:27–29). What Peter says is correct, of course. Yet, just as quickly as Peter announces that Jesus is the Messiah, Jesus "strictly ordered" his disciples not to repeat Peter's answer to anyone—no one is to be told that Jesus is the Messiah.

Now what kind of evangelistic outreach program is that?! If the very aim of the apostolic mission authorized by Jesus is to proclaim Jesus as the Messiah, why silence the disciples in proclaiming as much? It makes sense to rebuke and silence the unclean spirits that cry out, "You are the Son of God" (1:25, 34; 3:11–12; cf. 1:43)—what messiah would want to have his identity revealed by the opposing side? That might lead to skeptics charging that one's power and authority are really from Satan (3:22–27). But why silence your own followers? How is the world to come to receive salvation if the identity of the Messiah is not to be revealed by the Messiah's own disciples? Is this even the right question? Perhaps we should ask: What *kind* of messiah is the apostolic mission to proclaim? We might just as well ask: *Does* Peter truly confess the Messiah? Or, rather, in saying that Jesus is the Messiah, *which messiah* does Peter confess? And is that the Messiah the apostolic mission is to proclaim? This is revealed shortly in the narrative, to which we shall return.

Distancing from Jesus

In order to see in stark relief what sort of messiah it is that Peter actually confesses, it will be illuminating to see what sort of messiah it is that Peter eventually denies. For, in truth, Peter's confession is his denial, and his denial is his confession.

Peter's full denial of Jesus comes on the third stroke. At first, he denies only that he understands what the servant girl is asking him: "'You also were with Jesus, the man from Nazareth.' But he denied it, saying, 'I do not know or understand what you are talking about'" (14:67–68). On the second instance, he denies only being "one of them," one of those who were "with Jesus" (14:69–70). That is, he does not deny Jesus directly; rather, he denies association with those others who are identified with Jesus. Up to this point he has not disclaimed or disowned Jesus himself—he has only disclaimed understanding what he has been asked and dissociated himself

The Call to Follow

from Jesus' followers. In the third instance, however, Peter denies Jesus directly: "I do not know this man you are talking about" (14:71).

In denying Jesus, Peter speaks the truth: in truth, Peter does *not know* Jesus, "this man," *this* Messiah. The very one he has earlier confessed as Messiah, he does not truly know. And in denying Jesus, Peter makes his true confession.

At first, Peter distances himself from the question; then he distances himself from the other disciples. At last he distances himself from Jesus; and it is this distancing from Jesus that characterizes Peter's failure to know the Messiah. Peter's lack of knowledge is revealed by a failure of following, by the opening up of a separation between himself and Jesus. Before Peter reveals his separation from Jesus in word by way of his denial, his actions have already revealed his separation. When the servant girl puts Peter on trial, he is not with Jesus. In fact, that he is *not now* with Jesus creates the opportunity for the accusation, "You also *were* with Jesus." Had Peter stayed beside Jesus at *his* trial, had Peter remained "with Jesus," the question of association would have been obviated. It is because there has opened up a distance between Peter and Jesus that the question of association is made possible: Peter's dissociation from Jesus leaves Peter vulnerable to trial. Having left Jesus to his trial, Peter undergoes his own trial. We can observe Peter's separation by degrees from Jesus by retracing in reverse the narrative of Jesus' final hours—from the arrest, to the vigil, to the Supper.

Peter's distance from Jesus widens into a gulf at Jesus' arrest in the garden: "They took Jesus ... Peter followed at a distance" (14:53–54). Peter follows "at a distance" from Jesus precisely because he cannot follow closely a Messiah that is arrested, a Messiah who is taken prisoner "as though a bandit" (14:48). Peter's denial of the Messiah on trial begins in his dissociation from the Messiah that is "handed over," seized, arrested, and led away. Not only Peter dissociates from Jesus; none of the twelve—*none*—find themselves able to associate with one arrested as a criminal: "All of them deserted him and fled" (14:50). Denial is rooted in disloyalty: what Peter later confesses by word, he first discloses in action. Peter's desertion, his distant following of Jesus, originally reveals that he does "not know this man."

By disassociating himself from Jesus, by his act of disloyalty, Peter distances himself from both the identity and fate of Jesus. Indeed, these are the same—Jesus' fate of rejection is premised upon his identity as the Messiah, and Jesus' suffering and death on a cross reveals his identity, as

I Do Not Know this Man—A Disciple's Confession

we shall see. Now, Peter has pledged his undying loyalty to Jesus, even in death. Jesus told the disciples on the Mount of Olives, "You will all become deserters." Peter protests: "Even though all become deserters, I will not." Jesus then tells Peter that "this very night … you will deny me three times." Peter protests all the stronger, "Even though I must die with you, I will not deny you" (14:27–31). Peter's sincere pledge, though he cannot live up to its demands (not at this point), does reveal the truth about knowing Jesus: to know Jesus one must remain loyal to Jesus, and loyalty to Jesus entails solidarity with the Messiah in rejection, suffering, and death. Peter cannot muster this solidarity (not at this point); and because he cannot muster solidarity with Jesus he cannot but follow "at a distance," leaving himself vulnerable to the interrogator.

No sooner than Peter's confident pledge of undying loyalty has left his lips, a pledge repeated by all the twelve (14:31), Peter's solidarity with Jesus begins to slip: he, along with James and John, fails in keeping prayerful vigil with Jesus in the garden (14:32–42). Three times Jesus exhorts them to "watch and pray," and three times they fall away from Jesus into sleep. If they cannot remain united to Jesus in vigil, how will they identify with Jesus in arrest and trial, much less participate with Jesus in torture and execution? Before he can deny Jesus-on-trial, before even a distance opens between himself and Jesus-under-arrest, Peter's solidarity with Jesus-in-prayer has already slipped. Peter's separation from the fate of Jesus in the garden presages his failure under interrogation to identify with Jesus. At the very moment Jesus agonizes over, and willingly accepts, his fate, "this cup," as God's will (14:36), Peter cannot willingly keep himself awake in prayerful solidarity. Jesus thus rebukes Peter, warning him that his own trial is near: "'Simon, are you asleep? Could you not keep awake one hour? Keep awake and pray that you may not come into the time of trial'" (14:37–38).

All of this follows immediately upon the disciples having shared Eucharist with Jesus (14:22–25). During the Passover meal, Jesus "took a loaf of bread, and after blessing it he broke it, gave it to them, and said, 'Take; this is my body.'" Likewise, he "took a cup, and after giving thanks he gave it to them, and all of them drank from it. He said to them, 'This is my blood of the covenant, which is poured out for many.'" The disciples have all now shared in the bread of Jesus' body and the cup of Jesus' blood, by which sharing they signify their participation in the suffering and death of Jesus. Partaking of the one bread and the one cup signifies solidarity with Jesus in his fate as the Messiah. Afterward, on the Mount of Olives, as we saw,

The Call to Follow

the disciples do put their words to these symbols of suffering and death of which they have partaken, pledging loyalty to Jesus to the end, even unto death. But they cannot (not at this point) muster action to fulfill their pledge, they are not able to put flesh to their words, to substantiate the signs of solidarity in suffering and death: "All of them deserted him and fled."

More than this, by denying Jesus under interrogation Peter discloses that he has not fully grasped the significance of Jesus' words, "This is my body … This is my blood." Jesus' words, taken together with the signs of bread and cup, disclose Jesus' fate as the Messiah, the very fate ("this cup") over which Jesus agonizes in the garden while Peter snoozes. Peter thinks that because he has partaken of the one bread and the one cup in the ritual meal that he has expressed his solidarity with Jesus, that he thus has actually shared in Jesus' body and blood. But truly sharing in the body and blood of Jesus, signified by the bread and the cup, entails sharing the fate of the Messiah. Thus, Peter's first disclaimer to the servant-girl would seem to have been an apropos response also to Jesus' words: "I do not know or understand what you are talking about."

Ironically, Judas, the one who betrays Jesus, is the only one of the twelve who does not deny Jesus. At the Passover supper, Jesus had announced to the disciples, "Truly I tell you, one of you will betray me, one who is eating with me." The disciples each distance themselves from Jesus' charge of disloyalty: "Surely, not I?" Significantly, Jesus does not reveal the identity of the betrayer to the company of the disciples (14:17–21). It could be any one of them; and that lingering doubt over the identity of the betrayer likely strengthens their need later to pledge their lives in defense of their honor against Jesus' charge that they will all become deserters. The insubstantiality of those sincere pledges, and the truth of Jesus' charge, is revealed even as the betrayer is revealed and Jesus is betrayed. Judas had given the arresting crowd a sign: "The one I will kiss is the man" (14:44). By a single act—a sign of love and fidelity—Judas betrays Jesus to the arresting crowd, reveals himself as the betrayer to the company of disciples, and occasions the desertion of the rest of the disciples. In betraying Jesus—and here is the irony—Judas does what Peter later cannot muster himself to do: he identifies Jesus, saying by the kiss, "I know Jesus, and this is the man. I know this man, and he is Jesus." But although Judas *identifies* Jesus, Judas no more than Peter identifies *with* Jesus. Indeed, that is precisely the sense of his betrayal: Judas delivers Jesus over to a fate of suffering and death in which Judas will not himself share (in contrast with Matthew and Luke, Mark does not tell of Judas' fate).

Beginning from the unity of the Eucharist, we thus see a differentiating of the disciples from Jesus, a distancing foreshadowed by Jesus' announcement of a betrayer among them and the disciples' disclaimer, "Surely, not I?" It will be all of them before morning light. First, Jesus announces that, though one would betray him, all would desert him. Then, in reply to Peter's protest of loyalty, Jesus tells him that he will deny him. Then Peter, James, and John fall away from Jesus' fate during his hours of agony in the garden, slipping from vigilance into sleep, from undying loyalty into unguarded slumber. Then Judas betrays Jesus, and so commences the scattering of the sheep that Jesus prophesies: "You will all become deserters; for it is written, 'I will strike the shepherd, and the sheep will be scattered'" (14:27).

At this crucial juncture in the story, the disciples make a desperate, futile attempt to identify with Jesus, to share in his fate, to defend his life with their own lives as they had all pledged to do. But even by this attempt, they only separate themselves further from Jesus. One of the disciples—likely representing all of them (he is unnamed in the synoptic tradition, identified as Peter only in John's Gospel)—draws a sword and assaults the high priest's servant (14:47). Interestingly, unlike in the other synoptic accounts (cf. Matt 26:51–52; Luke 22:50–51), in Mark's telling Jesus does not rebuke his disciple for striking out in violence. It does not really require verbal rebuke—the act of violence rebukes itself. For the act of striking out in violence to defend the Messiah from arrest reveals that the one who draws the sword does not truly know the Messiah he sets out to defend. There is no communion between partaking of the bread and cup, sharing in the body and blood of Jesus, and drawing the sword, striking the body and shedding the blood of another.

Indeed, drawing the sword aims precisely at avoiding the fate signified by the bread and cup, the fate of suffering and death, the fate of the cross. To identify with *this* Messiah entails willing solidarity in suffering and death; solidarity with the to-be-crucified Messiah calls for renouncing the sword. By drawing the sword, the disciple falsifies his earlier pledge of loyalty to Jesus unto death; for by drawing the sword, the disciple shows himself willing, not to die with Jesus, but to kill in the name of Jesus—and that is no less than betrayal and desertion of the Messiah. One cannot identify with the Messiah through violence, not even with violence that appears to be justified in defense of the innocent.

The Call to Follow

Drawing the sword reveals the weakness of the flesh even more than does falling asleep while on watch in the garden vigil (14:38). To take up the sword in defense of the cause of the Messiah thus reveals one's own human weakness, one's own fear of suffering and death. To take up the sword is to abandon trust in the God who saves, the God unto whom Jesus surrenders his own life in the garden while awaiting arrest: "yet, not what I want, but what you want" (14:36). Thus it is that the sword-strike is already desertion, already denial of the to-be-crucified Messiah; the fleeing of the disciples, and the equivocating of Peter, are only the inevitable, tragic results of that fateful act. The disciple's sword-strike not only cuts off the ear of the high priest's servant; it severs the disciples from Jesus. Following this desperate act of violence, the twelve desert Jesus: "All of them deserted him and fled" (14:50).

Now that the drawing of the sword has undeniably disclosed the weakness of the flesh to follow Jesus, the twelve decisively separate themselves from the Messiah's fate. Peter, as we have seen, follows "at a distance." And this physical separation widens into a separation of identity. Unable to follow Jesus, Peter cannot identify with him: "I do not know this man." With this word of denial, the twelve have completely abandoned Jesus. The contingent of women disciples who had faithfully supported Jesus in Galilee and had followed him to Jerusalem—including Mary Magdalene, Mary the mother of James and Joses, and Salome, among others—do witness the crucifixion; but even these were "looking on from a distance" (15:40–41). Jesus shares his fate, not with any of his disciples, but only with the two "bandits" crucified with him (15:27). Jesus' sense of existential isolation in his messianic fate—signified by his distancing himself from the disciples as he prays in the garden (Mark 14:35, 39)—climaxes on the cross: "My God, my God, why have you forsaken me?" (15:34).

Facing Jesus

Even in his apparent abandonment by all, even as Jesus suffered his fate as Messiah in absence of friendly solidarity, one Roman centurion "stood facing him" (15:39). One of the enemy, one of his torturers and executioners, "stood facing him." While the women stood "looking from a distance," this one Roman centurion "stood facing him." Ironically, the only human to face Jesus as he dies is the very one responsible for carrying out his death sentence; the only one who faces Jesus as he suffers his fate as Messiah is the executioner of that fate. The centurion's fate is in an odd way bound up with Jesus' fate as Messiah. Executing Jesus' death sentence is the centurion's duty; to fulfill his duty, he must make sure of Jesus' death—to fail in his duty might mean death for himself. And in this ironic solidarity of executioner and condemned, the truth is disclosed for all to know by the centurion's exclamation: "Truly, this man was God's Son!" (15:39). Deepening the irony is the fact that the centurion unwittingly answers the very trial question put to Jesus by the high priest and affirms the very "blasphemy" for which Jesus is condemned by the Sanhedrin: "Are you the Messiah, the Son of the Blessed One?" (14:61–64).

The centurion evidently knows what the chief priests and scribes do not know despite all their scholarly knowledge of the sacred scriptures and all the testimony of many supposed eyewitnesses. And he knows this not merely because he witnesses Jesus' death; the chief priests and the scribes also witness Jesus' death and take opportunity to mock and deride him. The centurion knows the truth only because he stands *facing* Jesus hanging from the cross. The centurion's exclamation is the only unqualified disclosure of Jesus' identity in the entirety of Mark's Gospel, the only time a character discloses Jesus' identity and is not censured or silenced by Jesus. The centurion's exclamation is neither censured nor silenced, of course, precisely because Jesus has already died on the cross (15:37). The cross is the certification that the centurion's exclamation is true: suffering death on a cross certifies Jesus as Messiah, Son of God.

The chief priests and scribes say they would believe if only Jesus would come down from the cross and save himself: "He saved others; he cannot save himself. Let the Messiah, the King of Israel, come down from the cross now, so that we may see and believe" (15:31–32). They neither understand what they say nor know him of whom they speak anymore than Peter understood what he said when confessing Jesus as the Messiah. For the only messiah to be believed is the Messiah hanging crucified before their eyes. Their criterion for knowing the messiah is not much different from the disciples'; for they also cannot identify with the Messiah who suffers defenselessly a shameful death at human hands. The messiah of the chief priests and scribes, like that of the disciples, is one vindicated by force, a messiah who strikes out at his persecutors and takes retribution on his enemies to defend his honor and save himself from an ignominious fate. And, just as the disciples' drawing of the sword separated them from the Messiah's fate, so also does the chief priests' and scribes' mocking of Jesus disclose the distance between them and the purpose of God in revealing the Messiah.

The Call to Follow

Knowing Jesus' identity as the Messiah requires coming face-to-face with Jesus on a cross.

Denying Jesus

Thus it was that Peter's so-called confession of Jesus as the Messiah was actually a denial. As soon as Peter had proclaimed that Jesus is the Messiah, Jesus instructs Peter and the disciples just what this means and how it is that the Messiah is to be revealed to the world. For these are the same: the Messiah's mode of being revealed to the world discloses not only who the Messiah is (viz., Jesus) but also *what* it means to *be* the Messiah, what *kind* of savior the Messiah is to be. And, Jesus tells them, the Messiah will be definitively and decisively revealed—neither by Jesus saving himself so that others might believe in him, nor by the disciples spreading the message that Jesus is the Messiah—but rather through the rejection, torture, murder, and resurrection of the Messiah himself (8:31). All this Jesus says "quite openly" (8:32); and Jesus repeats this same message to his disciples twice more on the way to Jerusalem (9:31; 10:33–34). This, then, is the message that the disciples are to communicate about Jesus, the message that requires no censure: not that Jesus is the Messiah, but that the "Son of Man" will be arrested, executed—and raised again.

Peter will hear nothing of this. He takes Jesus aside and begins to "rebuke" him (8:32)! As Jesus had earlier censured the unclean spirits that proclaim him "the Holy One of God" (1:24–25, 34), Peter now censures Jesus, the one he has just confessed as Messiah, the Anointed One of God. Had Peter truly confessed Jesus as Messiah, he would not now be rebuking him. We thus should ask: What sort of messiah did Peter confess? Evidently, what Jesus discloses about being the Messiah is incompatible with the messiah Peter has just confessed; evidently, Peter did not mean to confess a rejected, suffering, dying Messiah.

It would seem that the messiah Peter confesses is of the dominating rather than the dying sort, one who comes in conquering power and overwhelming victory, decisively crushing the enemies of God. The true Messiah *does* come in power and victory, only not the all-too-human power and victory that Peter imagines. Instead of gaining victory over the powers by dominating his enemies, by crushing those who would reject him, this Messiah is to be crushed in apparent defeat by the powers that oppose him. Peter, however, cannot confess a crushed and (apparently) defeated

I Do Not Know this Man—A Disciple's Confession

Messiah. And so Jesus rebukes Peter before the rest of the disciples: "Get behind me, Satan!" By his confession and rebuke, Peter has revealed himself as the opposition—Satan! Instead of confessing Jesus as the Messiah, Peter has effectively rejected the Messiah. And he does so because he confesses a messiah according to the pattern of human thinking rather than a Messiah according to the pattern of divine purpose: "You are setting your mind not on divine things but on human things" (8:33).

This all-too-human understanding of the messiah, against which Jesus warns the disciples, stands behind the disciples' drawing the sword in defense of Jesus in the garden. It is a messiah who conquers by force and rules by domination that one defends by force, not the Messiah that wills to obey God to the utmost, even to the point of accepting defeat in weakness and suffering death in dishonor. Peter confesses the popular messiah, the messiah desired by the crowds, the messiah given birth by popular resentment against the Roman occupation. Aware that not only the disciples but many in the crowds following him share Peter's all-too-human messianic expectation, Jesus begins to teach them what it means to be a disciple, what it means to follow him, to know *this* Messiah: "If any want to become my followers, let them deny themselves and take up their cross and follow me" (8:34). To know Jesus as the Messiah, to be able to truly confess that Jesus is the Messiah, entails that one follow Jesus; and following Jesus entails no less than sharing the fate of the Messiah, participating in the Messiah's suffering and death. Authentically identifying with Jesus as his disciple requires solidarity with the cross—and thus renouncing the sword.

So it is that Peter does not really confess Jesus as Messiah, but confesses only the popular expectation of what a messiah should be and do. So it is that Peter cannot accept (not yet) the rejected Messiah; and so it will be that Peter will reject the Messiah he cannot accept. Thus it was that Peter's denial is his true confession: "I do not know this man." What the experience of Peter (and the other disciples) teaches us is this: to confess any messiah other than the One revealed to the world hanging on a cross is not true confession, but only self-deception and, ultimately, denial of the truth and hostile resistance to God. It is only by solidarity with Jesus in the way of the cross that one can truly know who the Messiah is and what kind of salvation the Messiah is to bring. Following Jesus in the way of the cross and truly knowing Jesus as Messiah are inseparable.

Confessing Jesus

Before Jesus could be authentically proclaimed as Messiah by the apostles, Jesus had to demonstrate what that proclamation truly means: because Jesus is the Messiah, to "proclaim Christ" can be nothing other than to proclaim "Christ crucified" (1 Cor 1:23; 2:2). Thus, the church's apostolic confession of Jesus as Messiah, Lord and Savior, had to be *lived out in the flesh* by Jesus in the face of an uncomprehending and hostile world before it could be authentically proclaimed in word by the church to the world. The corollary is that, in order to sustain its true confession of Jesus as Messiah and Son of God, in order to authenticate its proclamation of Christ to the world, the *church* also must *live out* its confession *in the flesh* before an uncomprehending and hostile world. In order to confess truly that Jesus is Messiah and Lord, in order to proclaim authentically Christ crucified, the church must *be* the body of Christ—suffering, rejected, crucified, and resurrected. Otherwise, the church's proclamation is only as credible as Peter's confession.

The message of a church that knows nothing of suffering and persecution—that does not take up its cross—is not to be believed. A church that distances itself from the suffering of the poor and oppressed is a church that, like Peter, follows Jesus only "at a distance." A church that has made itself acceptable to the powers that be and stands comfortable with the status quo by "warming [itself] at the fire" alongside the guardians of this present darkness (Mark 14:54) is a church that falsifies the gospel it preaches. A church whose gospel sanctions structures of oppression and systems of domination is a church that, like Peter, denies Jesus: "I do not know this man." Like Peter, the church cannot both identify with Jesus as the betrayed, arrested, tortured, and executed Messiah and at the same time identify with those who align themselves against Christ by oppressing the weak and exploiting the vulnerable. The church cannot in truth collaborate with the powers that crush the poor and rob the needy and claim to be the body of Christ, whose own body was crushed by those same powers.

The church cannot truly confess Jesus as Messiah and Lord unless it identifies with and shares the fate of the broken victims, those in our world today who are being crucified by the powers that be. The necessary corequisite of true confession and authentic proclamation of Jesus as Messiah and Lord is solidarity with the poor and oppressed, with those who suffer rejection, persecution, false accusation, disappearance and secret detention, imprisonment, torture, and execution. It is not adequate for the church to proclaim a crucified and risen Lord: only a crucified and risen church—only a church that knows both suffering and rejection by the world and renewal and restoration by God, only a church that knows by cross and resurrection a foretaste of the coming victory of God's kingdom over the rulers of the present world age—can authentically proclaim the gospel. Just as the cross certifies Jesus as the Messiah, the cross certifies the church as the body of Christ.

Jesus' rebuke of Peter entails that we cannot substitute confession of Jesus as Messiah and Son of God for identifying with Jesus in persecution and rejection. Furthermore, that Jesus warns his disciples of betrayal just prior to sharing Eucharist with them, and that he warns his disciples of desertion under trial just after sharing Eucharist with them, makes clear to us that we cannot substitute symbolic participation in the bread and cup for real participation in the suffering and death of Jesus: we cannot separate solidarity in the ritual of communion from solidarity in the reality of the cross. Wherever the church fails to share in the passion of those disciples today who are rejected and persecuted for identifying with Jesus, who suffer and die for the sake of following Jesus, there the church knows no communion with Christ, there the church confesses Christ falsely. The church that is founded upon Peter's confession of a popular messiah, a church that is a stranger to the way of the cross, is nothing other than a false witness to Christ—to which Jesus says as he did to Peter: "Get behind me, Satan!"

The Valley of Shadows

*Even though I walk
through the valley of the shadow of death,
I fear no evil;
for you are with me . . .*
—Psalm 23:4

*This was to fulfill what had been spoken
through the prophet Isaiah,
"He took our infirmities and bore our diseases."*
—Matthew 8:17

*"And remember,
I am with you always,
to the end of the age."*
—Matthew 28:20

4

The Way Home—
A Disciple's Reclamation

I wait for the LORD, *my soul waits,*
and in his word I hope;
my soul waits for the LORD
more than those who watch for the morning,
more than those who watch for the morning.

—PSALM 130:5–6

Before making the commitment to follow Jesus, I spent a period of five years, 1990–1995, wandering in the spiritual wilderness, a self-chosen exile in which I searched for a way of salvation apart from Christ and the church. This project of self-reliance eventually turned into a bondage to self that emptied me of hope, a slavery to the fear that the existentialist philosophers called "angst"— the fear of (being) nothing. This piece recounts, through a series of poems, my experience of exile and redemption. Despite my doubts, Jesus walked with me through the valley of fear and led me to an oasis of grace. When I could not see the way for myself, Jesus sent faithful friends to accompany me and show me the way home—back to Christ, and back to the church.

I have called my return from exile "reclamation." This term is borrowed from Charles Dickens' A Christmas Carol, a story that captured my imagination as a young adult and which I would read at Christmastime during the years prior to my exile (and the various film versions of which I still enjoy watching). When the first night visitor, the Ghost of Christmas Past, appears to Scrooge disrupting his sleep, he inquires what business has brought her to him. The Spirit replies, "Your welfare!"—but sensing that he was thinking that a night of uninterrupted sleep would be more beneficial, she restates her purpose: "Your reclamation, then. Take heed!" In my personal copy, now yellowed by years, that phrase—"Your reclamation"—is underlined. At some level, even at that point in my life, I was identifying with Scrooge's nighttime passage through the shadows of his life to the morning of hope and joy.

The narrative portions here are adapted from my reflection, "Surprised by joy," published originally in The Mennonite *(2011).*

～

Exile

For several years during my twenties I was, literally and figuratively, lost. I was one of those who sit in darkness beneath the shadow of fear, waiting for the Lord, waiting for the morning. Having wandered from the church, I was walking alone the shadowy vale.

I had been raised in a Christian home, where I was read Bible stories on my mother's lap and we held daily family devotions. Our family went to church every Sunday (twice!), where I was taught "the faith of our fathers" and I was baptized a "believer" while yet a young child. At age thirteen, on graduation from eighth grade, I received a card from a family close to ours. In it the father, Harvey, had written this note: "May the great Triune God be enough for thee."

At the time I wanted so much for that to be true, but I wasn't sure I could simply say "yes" to it. Even as a youth I had a complex, inquisitive mind and tended to asked questions—too many for my parents' comfort. Looking back, I think that Harvey, who knew me well, recognized that it would be a struggle for me to be satisfied with the simplicity of faith.

Now I was in college and, like most young adults, I wanted to chart my own course—in life and in faith. I didn't want to reject God, or even Christianity. At the same time I couldn't accept God on the fundamentalist terms of the Christianity I had known as a child.

The Way Home—A Disciple's Reclamation

So, I went off in quest of my own salvation—to work out salvation for myself, by myself. I read the ancient philosophers, the existentialist writers, even books on Zen Buddhism. I cultivated solitude in an effort to be "authentic." I wrote poetry to express and embrace the "fear and trembling" of a lone pilgrim on an unmarked path.

> Am I to remain a meaningless joke forever?
> When is my laughter?
> Is hope ever to rise again from the ashes of despair?
> Is all to remain dreary and dreadful?
>
> A cavernous dark envelops me.
> I cannot discern direction.
> I step but know not where,
> I stumble over what I cannot see,
> I am pierced by what I cannot feel.
>
> My eyes have withered,
> My heart failed.
> I fall to my hands and knees
> To feel my way,
> But the ground beneath me
> Crumbles and gives way.
>
> How long will I fall,
> How far down is bottom?
> Is there bottom?
>
> Has my sun set forever,
> Leaving me to wander alone in the weary night?
> But so also is night a sun.

I eventually came to the conclusion that it would not be enough for me to pull myself up out of nothingness and will an authentic life—to declare, however sincerely, that "night is a sun." To truly live I needed not only to be free from fear but also from guilt. Beyond that, I needed to know that love was real and that there was something to hope for. All this, however, I could not do for myself—indeed, it was my "self" that needed saving. This depiction of my personal struggle to overcome fear reflected my realization that the project of salvation by self-reliance was futile:

> Where has fear gone?
> I see it not but sense its presence—

The Valley of Shadows

> Stalking, ready to pounce with a fierce vengeance.
> Why does it refuse to show its face?
>
> Come out and show yourself!
> Step into the light so that nothing is hidden between us!
>
> I know you will lurk in the shadows,
> Waiting for me to sleep,
> So you can shatter my peace and
> Lay waste to my paradise.
>
> Your silent cowardice haunts me.
> My foolish courage stirs for a fleeting moment.
> I leap to strangle you
> But my spirit stumbles and falls.
> Confused in the impenetrable darkness,
> I scurry to the corner to hide.
>
> Kill me, kill me now!
> Wait no longer to release your anger!
> O fear, have mercy!
> Leave me alone so that I may suffer in solitude.
>
> But you are not so kind.
> Forever will you follow me.
> There is no escape,
> No salvation.

I was lost and I knew it, but I didn't know how to find the way back home. I began to pray through my poetry—for faith, for hope, for redemption. This was my final prayer:

> Anticipating that moment
> When the sign appears,
> When hope shows its face,
> When my sun rises again.
>
> But will my faith endure,
> Or will it waver and fail
> When that crucial time arrives?
>
> Or have I already lost my faith?
>
> Will I see that miraculous sign,
> Or will my eyelids droop heavy with doubt?

And if I do see it,
Will I possess the will to believe?
Will I trust enough to reach out and
Take hold of the promise?

The traditional spiritual tells my story: "When I was a seeker, I sought both night and day. I prayed the Lord to help me, and He showed me the way." Two years would pass, however, before I would see the first light of dawn.

Return

In the meantime, I had begun doctoral studies at the University of Notre Dame—where there's a crucifix in every classroom, Our Lady adorns the Golden Dome, and ten-story Touchdown Jesus flanks the library. In an ironic twist of divine providence, there in the midst of my self-chosen exile from the church I found myself surrounded by the church—the Catholic Church! The Catholic Church was the last place I would ever have expected to receive grace and find salvation—every instinct from my fundamentalist upbringing rebelled at the very thought of it.

My redemption from exile began one day in the summer after my first year. Deirdre, a fellow student, saw me eating lunch alone and invited me to join a group of her friends. Reluctantly, I did. She introduced me to Jeanne, Joan, and Tim.

I began joining them for lunch regularly and soon realized that these were not only people I wanted to know but were the friends that I needed. They had what I was longing for—faith and hope—and something more besides, joy. Yet, they were Catholics, devout Catholics. Wasn't Catholicism legalistic and graceless? How could they be both faithful Catholics and joyful people? At times I doubted what I was seeing was real.

Despite my doubts and fears, over the next two years these four friends led me back to faith and wooed me back to the church through the gentle love and gracious hospitality of genuine friendship. They were evangelical Catholics in the truest sense of "evangelical"—they believed the Christian faith was good news and that the church was home on earth, and so were intent on sharing their faith with others and inviting them to join the family of God.

Dawn broke clear on a Sunday morning in September. Light suffused the room, filling my heart and my head. In a moment, I was sure that God

The Valley of Shadows

was near and love was real; for I had seen both through my friends. Fear fled. Hope appeared. I recounted the beginning of my return from exile:

> Heaven opens wide its watchful eye upon a world waiting
> And with a caressing stroke shades the surrounding wilderness
> In muted hues brushed softly over fluid shapes.
> Earth yawns a lazy breeze
> That quietly rustles scrub brush scattered along the broken slopes.
> An unseen hand reaching out of nowhere
> Sweeps gently across my place in a sheltering cleft of rock
> And shakes me earnestly from unsettling sleep,
> Pointing my attention toward shadows receding from the valley below.
> Focusing through a dissipating haze,
> I see it uncovered by the growing light.
> I had not desired to see it here,
> Yet its appearing was a precious sight.
> I had not looked to see it now,
> Yet its appearing was in perfect season.
> My faith, nearly withered and almost failing, had endured
> The lingering night of oppressive absence
> That turns anticipation into agony and doubt into torment.
> My destitute soul had lived
> To see the promised completion of my only hope.
> What, though, had I waited to find?
> Is revealed before me my road to Canaan?
> Or simply my direction for today?
> Whither it leads I know not.
> But in confident trust will I follow without haunting fear.
> For the sign was made manifest and the way clear.

A couple of months later, as I slept one night, I received a vision that confirmed my faith in following the path before me. I dreamed that I was present at a gathering of friends, including the same ones who had walked with me the previous two years. The conversation in the room was abuzz with the news that a famous nun, the mother superior of a religious order, was visiting in the city and would be giving a talk that evening. My friends were getting ready to leave and go to hear her speak, and they encouraged me to come along with them. I declined their invitation, saying I would wait behind until they returned. After they had left, I felt drawn to go out onto the porch of the house, through which my friends had just left. As I stepped onto the porch, I sensed that someone was at the opposite end—I turned and saw a woman, dressed in full habit, arms crossed. At first I dropped my head in shame, confessing that I was sorry for not having gone with the others to see her. But then she extended her arms toward me in a wide arc, and with a compassionate expression beckoned me to come to her. Without hesitating, I went to her—and, speaking my name, she embraced me in love. I awoke. I was home.

5

Into Your Hands—
A Disciple's Requiem

Into your hand I commit my spirit;
you have redeemed me, O Lord, faithful God.
I will exult and rejoice in your steadfast love,
because you have seen my affliction;
you have taken heed of my adversities.
Be gracious to me, O Lord, for I am in distress;
my eye wastes away from grief, my soul and body also.
For my life is spent with sorrow, and my years with sighing;
my strength fails because of my misery, and my bones waste away.
I have passed out of mind like one who is dead;
I have become like a broken vessel.

—From Psalm 31

He has made my flesh and my skin waste away, and broken my bones;
he has besieged and enveloped me with bitterness and tribulation;
he has made me sit in darkness like the dead of long ago.
My soul is bereft of peace; I have forgotten what happiness is;
so I say, "Gone is my glory, and all that I had hoped for
from the Lord."

The Valley of Shadows

> *The thought of my affliction and my homelessness*
> *is wormwood and gall!*
> *My soul continually thinks of it and is bowed down within me.*
> *But this I call to mind, and therefore I have hope:*
> *The steadfast love of the* L<small>ORD</small> *never ceases,*
> *his mercies never come to an end;*
> *they are new every morning; great is your faithfulness.*
> *"The* L<small>ORD</small> *is my portion," says my soul, "therefore I will hope in him."*
> *The* L<small>ORD</small> *is good to those who wait for him,*
> *to the soul that seeks him.*
> *It is good that one should wait quietly*
> *for the salvation of the* L<small>ORD</small>.
>
> —F<small>ROM</small> L<small>AMENTATIONS</small> 3

John P. Kenny was a professor of mine who became a mentor and then a colleague and friend. John died of a brain tumor in 2004. It took a year and a half of dwelling with John's death until I had come to a place of peace with my grief. A church retreat in early Lent presented an opportunity to remember John while walking in the woods, during which the Holy Spirit told me it was time to write about John's dying. And so, a couple weeks later, I returned to the place where the Spirit had spoken in order to write a memoir of John.

Recalling those last months, walking with John through "the valley of the shadow of death," still readily brings tears to my eyes—tears of sorrow for loss and tears of joy for life. Were our way in this world only joy, it would be too sweet to savor; were our way in this world only sorrow, it would be too bitter to bear. But God has given us the bittersweet burden of walking together the way of both joy and sorrow, and Jesus has sent us the Holy Spirit to walk the way with us.

I wrote this memoir in the Thoreau House at The Hermitage near Three Rivers, Michigan, on 18 March and 14 April (Good Friday) 2006. While writing, I listened to recordings of the Requiem *by Wolfgang Amadeus Mozart and the* Requiem *by John Rutter.*

~

The not unexpected news arrived by email in early September 2004 in Klaipeda, Lithuania, where I had just begun an international service assignment with Mennonite Mission Network. John had passed away in late August. On the day of his memorial service in Peoria, Illinois, I went to the old city market in Klaipeda and bought a colorful bouquet of flowers, hand-picked and arranged by one of the babushkas there, to remember him. I then boarded the ferry to cross the narrow lagoon to the Curonian Spit, a slender strip of sand and trees that runs along the coast of the Baltic Sea. After disembarking, I trekked along the footpath through the birch woods across the spit to the white-sand, wind-sculpted beach. Facing west toward John's native Ireland, I read aloud to the sea the Yeats poem that would be read by his daughter at his memorial service.

Had someone asked John Kenny as he neared death the same question asked of Henry David Thoreau at the end of his life—whether he had made his peace with God—I expect that John would have given much the same reply as Thoreau: "I am not aware that we have ever quarreled." John, like Thoreau, was heterodox in his beliefs, to say the least, and it was not different at the end of his life. He believed in a cosmos and a God that most of us would find quite strange indeed—not the world we call home or the God we call "God." And that was because John, I think, was a mystic at heart—a visionary who taught physics and professed Catholicism, who saw poetry beneath the equations and mystery beyond the dogmas, a reality more real than we know, a truth that neither mathematics nor magisterium could ever articulate adequately.

One year earlier, in September 2003, I had received another email informing me that John was sick, possibly dying—a brain tumor. A sudden seizure had brought him close to death that spring. A follow-up examination revealed the tumor, already advanced to a stage beyond the point of surgical remedy and unlikely to respond to treatment.

It had been a few years since last I had seen John. I was an undergraduate physics student of his at Bradley University in the early 1990s. I asked him to be the faculty mentor for my senior research project; he agreed, and I was drawn into the "chaosmos" of John P. Kenny.[1] This was a domain that I'm sure the other faculty members realized was not necessarily the same reality taught in physics textbooks—a reality hiding many more possibilities than academic orthodoxy could ever acknowledge. This was evident in

---

1. *Chaosmos*, a term taken from James Joyce, is the title of the unpublished book that John P. Kenny wrote in the last years of his life.

the department seminars where John had professed his heterodoxy, putting forward an alternative model for elementary particles he'd been working on for a couple of decades. He was never satisfied with the conventional wisdom, persistently searching for a more ancient, more primitive understanding, a deeper insight into the nature of things. This insight, in the world of Kenny, could come from poetry as well as (or better than) physics. And being an Irishman, first and last, it would be for him the prose of Joyce and the verse of Yeats that proved most revelatory of reality.

At first I thought him eccentric—odd, but intriguingly so—and his interests in theoretical physics and in the history and philosophy of science fit well with my penchant for philosophical questions generated by my study of physics. That is why I sought to work with him on my senior project. He was at the beginning stage of a research program and invited me to work with him and see where it would go. And it would last for nearly a decade and produce no fewer than five published articles in professional journals—an outcome I would have thought unlikely at the start.

As we collaborated over the next several years while I was in graduate studies at the University of Notre Dame, John became both colleague and friend. I would come back to Bradley during fall and spring breaks and summer vacations for a week at a time so we could work together, generate and test ideas, work out equations, analyze results—and, at every step, ponder the significance of what we were doing, for both theoretical physics and the human understanding of the cosmos. In John's view, which I did not always share, we were developing a new way of understanding the nature of things; and at times it was both perplexing and exciting to witness what was taking shape in his imagination. It was one of the most intellectually fervent and satisfying periods of my life. It was also a time of intense spiritual searching for me.

During these visits, I was warmly welcomed to stay in the Kenny home. This afforded us opportunity for many conversations outside work—at breakfast (on the few occasions I was up in time to catch John before he left for the office), walking over to the university, over lunch, walking back home in the afternoon, over supper, and in the evening on the porch over a pot of tea or down at the pub over a pint of stout. Our conversations ranged the length and breadth of human concern: politics, economics, international affairs, ethics, philosophy, literature, and theology.

The news of John's illness struck me hard—how long since I'd seen him? I had not visited for three years. The last time I communicated with him was in the spring of 2002, to share with him the sad news that my dissertation director, Jim Cushing, had taken his own life after a long depression brought on by the onset of a slight cognitive deficit that only Jim could sense (and of which I, like many others, was unaware). Jim died on Good Friday, and I learned of his death via the newspaper on Saturday—but it wasn't until Easter Sunday morning, at church, that I learned his death had been suicide. That terrible news, on the very morning we heard the good news of resurrection, doubled me over in pain and confusion.

John had also known Jim. In fact, John had invited Jim to give some lectures at Bradley during my senior year in 1992. I not only met Jim at that time, but he gave me good advice about graduate studies and encouraged me to pursue what sustained my passion—all of which eventually led me to Notre Dame to do doctoral work in philosophy of physics with Jim. Oddly (or not so oddly, given John's ways), I didn't hear back from John after I'd emailed him about Jim. And now, the news that John might not live much longer, with the painful memory of Jim's untimely death still lingering.

My first instinct was to visit. I was living in South Bend, a four-hour drive from Peoria—too far for a day trip. The next opportunity would be the Thanksgiving holiday, when I would visit my parents, only a ninety-minute drive from Peoria. As the time neared, I called Pat, his wife, and arranged to visit the day after Thanksgiving. When I arrived, the house was full of their (adult) children and grandchildren and a few other visitors. It was good to see all of them again—and to find John sitting in his usual place in his favorite chair. I took my familiar spot in the rocking chair, and we began to chat.

Just like old times, I thought. But it wasn't old times. The signs of John's illness, and the effects of chemo- and radiation-therapy, soon became apparent: pasty skin, slumped posture, swollen belly, slight trembling in the hand, somewhat slurred speech, random lapses in memory.

We began by each catching the other up on what we had been doing the past few years, sharing news of personal acquaintances, discussing recent world events and the course of his treatment. I then asked him the question that had anxiously been on my mind since arriving—whether he had received my emails about Jim's death. The look of mortality flashed across his face as he labored a bit to remember. Yes, he had—a tragic thing, he said. It was an unnerving thing to ask a dying man about another man's death. And while we remembered Jim together, I wondered, but did not have the nerve to ask, whether John had ever contemplated making the same choice as Jim, to end his life. And this all the while his grandchildren were coming and going from the room, moving in and out of his attention and our conversation.

After we had chatted an hour or so, the Kennys' oldest daughter interrupted us and reminded him that they had planned to go to his office at the university that day to begin clearing out his books and other things. They invited me to go along. This was no small undertaking, as John could not walk on his own power. It was perhaps then, watching his daughter and son-in-law assisting him in and out of his wheelchair and the van, that his mortality, the frailty of his being, struck me.

Since I had visited last, the university had constructed a new addition to the science building, in which the physics department was now housed. Yet, while I had not been in this building before, and although it was no longer in the same room, I still recognized John's office, where I had spent many hours and days in researching, writing, and, best of all, conversing with John and others. The books, the artwork (including a print of Salvador Dali's stunning painting, *Christ of St. John of the Cross*, a framed print of which now hangs in my own office), the piles of papers, the desk clutter, the Moroccan sheepskin seat cover—all the same as before, but now appearing as relics of a past rather than vital signs of a man's work. John granted me the pick of books I wanted (a living bequest, of sorts), and as I surveyed the shelves I saw many familiar tomes—on more than just physics: history, theology, poetry, cosmology, archaeoastronomy, representing the many facets of John's soul. It was an honor, and a regret, to receive these books—to realize that, just as John's library was now being dismantled and dispersed, so too, soon, would be his intellect.

I resolved to redeem the time remaining. As I prepared to leave, John asked me if I would come and visit him again. I promised him I would. His eyes spoke what his words withheld. Already in our earlier conversation, I had sensed that there was not only much yet for us to talk about, but that he desired to be able to confront his mortality squarely rather than obliquely. He had said several times, after repeating his medical condition, treatment, and prognosis, "and that's about it for me." It seemed as though he meant to say—"That is the end and sum of my life." He believed that death was certainly and quickly approaching and didn't share the optimism of others that a miraculous remission of the cancer was possible. He needed to be able to say this openly and live with it honestly—and our conversation cleared a space within which he could do that. We said our goodbyes, he emphasizing that I should come again, I promising that I would return.

My next visit was on the afternoon of Christmas Eve. In contrast to the busyness of the Kenny house on Thanksgiving weekend, this day the house was quiet—the extended family would not be arriving until later that evening. In the absence of the distractions, my attention was able to focus more on John. But there would not be much verbal conversation between us that day. It was not a good day, he told me—the words were getting lost, the thoughts escaping. It was, he said, as if the words had to swim against the current of a viscous fluid to reach the world, and only a few bits of verbiage, sometimes not coherently connected, were getting through. Pat, his wife, said that some days John did better, others not so well, and there was no way to know what to expect from one day to the next. John's motor function and coordination were also weakening, leaving his hands shaky all the time. He was doing basic gripping and squeezing exercises with a soft ball to help maintain strength.

We sat in the sunroom off the back of the house watching European football on the TV, soccer being one of John's lifelong passions. I helped Pat serve him a simple lunch of oatmeal and toast. A couple of longtime friends of theirs stopped by to bring Christmas greetings and visit for a while, but John was unable to engage in the conversation. After all this, John had grown tired and needed to take a nap. So, after saying goodbyes and exchanging Christmas peace with John and Pat, I took my leave, promising to visit again as soon as I could—not knowing whether John would live until that time or, if he did, whether he would be able to think and speak clearly enough on that day for us to talk. I wondered whether we had had our last talk.

Meanwhile, I was participating in a Sunday school class on developing habits of sharing faith with others in everyday circumstances "with gentleness and reverence" (1 Pet 3:16). One simple habit we learned was to prepare for a conversation with someone (whether in person or by phone) by praying for that person and inviting the presence of God in the conversation. Another habit we learned was paying attention to places or moments in a conversation where the other person seems open to talking of spiritual things, especially where the other broaches the subject, so it would not seem intrusive to speak or ask concerning God. We would introduce one new habit each Sunday, practice it throughout the week, and then report back to the group what had happened the following Sunday. We were also praying with and for each other concerning relationships—with family, friends, neighbors, or coworkers—where we were already sharing our faith or looking for opportunities to do so. It was coming near the end

The Valley of Shadows

of the Sunday school quarter when my next visit with John was planned, in late January. I became aware that the Holy Spirit was leading me to speak directly with John about ultimate things—God and death. I related this to my class the Sunday before my visit and we prayed for God to open the opportunity.

As I sat in the car outside the Kenny home that Friday afternoon, not knowing whether John would be lucid or not, I paused before going in, praying for John and for the presence of the Holy Spirit, and for the vision and courage to see and seize the moment. Inside I found that, except for his younger son, who was caring for him that afternoon, John was home alone and had just woken from a nap. He was still lying down in his hospital bed, set up in the living room. I went in and pulled up to his bedside the rocking chair that I had often occupied during our many conversations over the years. To my relief and joy, it was a good day for John—he was clear-headed and eager to talk. Pat had told him I was coming and he was expecting me. I adjusted his bed and pillows so he could sit up as we talked. And we talked . . .

He reveled in telling me about his youngest daughter's trip to Ireland for a wedding—and I could hear in his voice and see in his face love for his homeland and longing for one more journey home. I had once imagined, and we had often talked, of one day me joining him and his family for a holiday in Ireland. I excitedly told him that I was now for sure going to Lithuania to teach, and his enthusiasm was evident as we talked about where my life might be going next. He was sure I would meet a Lithuanian woman, get married, and settle down there. (As it turns out, he was not far off—I would end up getting engaged in Lithuania, but to a Canadian woman, then getting married in Canada, and settling back in the United States!)

He was also eager to share with me a vision he'd had one night—a dream about where his life would be going next. In the dream there was a light that revealed to him that death is not the end, a cessation of existence, but upon death we are transformed into another, higher mode of existence. This confirmed for him what he already believed, an idea he had long pondered and researched in physics, but still rather heterodox. Even now we exist within a higher-dimensional reality than we can sense; there is more to reality than what we can know scientifically and experience bodily. We ourselves are shadow realities projected from a higher dimension. Bodily existence limits our experience to four-dimensional space-time; death frees us to a higher-dimensional existence unbounded by space and time: that is, upon death we exist in *more* than just four dimensions—we exist *five*-dimensionally. That is an idea our cave-dwelling minds simply cannot comprehend, but the light of his dream had given John a glimpse of this higher dimensional existence, an existence equations and dogmas cannot contain. At the beginning of the book he wrote at the end of his life, John writes: "We humans cry for a vision, for an audible whisper of wisdom that tells us what we are doing in this chaosmos. We act for the most part like autistic children that understand what is going on but are unable to articulate any explanation."[2] John had at long last received "an audible whisper of wisdom" from the chaosmos, and it was clear that this vision had given him hope and peace in facing his approaching death.

I now believe that this vision was given to him by God, to deliver him from fear of dying and so to free him to allow events to take their course. And it was here that I saw the opening prepared by the Holy Spirit. Without hesitating to think of the right thing to say, as I opened my mouth the right words came out: "So, do you sense that all of this is in God's hands?" From there we talked on quite awhile about ultimate things. During the course of the conversation, we returned again to the ending of Jim's life. John said that he had contemplated long on the way his life would end—and on the temptation to take that into his own hand. But he had resolved that he would not do that—if only because of the joy he took in his grandchildren and because so many family and friends cared about him and were willing him to live. He was not yet done living.

When it seemed as though we had reached a concluding point, John said, "Well then, do you want to pray?" I was pleasantly surprised: in all the years we had known each other, we had never once prayed together, and I would never have expected John to invite me to pray. I said I'd be glad to pray with him. I reached out my hand, and he joined his hand to mine. I first gave thanks and praise to God for the gift of another day of life and then gave thanks for the gift of John's life and for the gift he had been to the lives of so many others. I prayed that God would sustain John's life with joy and grant him rest from his fears and fill him with hope and courage. I then commended John's life into God's hands . . . but, before I could finish, John cut me off with an abrupt and loud "Amen!" followed by the playful editorial comment, "You Protestants always pray too long!" We shared a hearty laugh and shed a few tears.

---

2. Kenny, *Chaosmos*, chapter 1 (quoted by permission).

The Valley of Shadows

Soon after this, Pat returned home from her errands and it was time for John to rest. As John and I said our goodbyes, I promised to return around Easter. Sitting in the car outside, I paused to praise God for prayer more than answered. And I prayed what would become my daily prayer for the next seven months: "Lord, I commend John's life into your hands this day."

The next morning, sitting in bed at my parent's home, I neared the end of my regular morning prayer, following *The Book of Common Prayer*, and came to the place for the collect of the day and prayer for mission. The BCP includes three prayers for mission in the morning rite, which I used in no particular order. That day, without forethought, I chose the third:

> Lord Jesus Christ, you stretched out your arms of love on the hard wood of the cross that everyone might come within the reach of your saving embrace: So clothe us in your Spirit that we, reaching forth our hands in love, may bring those who do not know you to the knowledge and love of you; for the honor of your Name. Amen.[3]

Remembering the day before with John, our hands joined as we prayed, I wept and rejoiced.

I visited next on Good Friday. John was sleeping when I arrived, and Pat was the only other one there. She was working in the kitchen, busily preparing food for the family feasting that was to come over the Easter holiday. We took the opportunity to chat awhile, I sitting at the table sipping a cup of tea, she chopping vegetables at the counter and cooking at the stove. She welcomed my company and talked freely about John's prognosis and treatment—and the financial hardship all this had brought them into. I marveled at her graceful strength and faith in God to sustain and provide: "God will get us through this." I told her I had been praying for her and John and the rest of the family, and she thanked me—"We'll take all the prayer we can get!"

After some time we heard John stirring in his bed in the living room and Pat went to check on him. He was awake, so, while Pat returned to the kitchen, I helped him out of bed and into his wheelchair and wheeled him into the sun room, where I helped him into his easy chair. We began talking, and before long it was clear that his thought and speech had diminished significantly since I had last seen him. And Pat confirmed that there were now more bad days than good. But I did sense that John's spirit

---

3. *Book of Common Prayer*, 101.

was more alive than before. Soon some family members arrived for their weekend visit, and we all chatted for an hour or so. After taking my leave, as I began driving back to my parent's home, I was giving thanks for the opportunity God had given us to share deeply about ultimate things.

My next, and last, visit was in May. I knew going there that day it would be my last time to see John—in a few months I would be leaving for Lithuania and had a busy summer of preparation ahead of me. John was awake and in his chair in the sun room when I arrived. Pat and a few other family members were there also and we chatted together. John was no longer able to express complex thoughts or complete coherent sentences of much more than a few words. This, of course, was quite frustrating for him; even so, he was by no means willing to resign himself to silence. Also, his motor function and hand coordination had seriously deteriorated—the soft toys he had once used to strengthen his hands lay unused on the table beside his chair. Since our conversation in January, I was more comfortable just being with him, without the sense of needing our visit to be about something.

The conversation eventually came around to my approaching teaching mission to Lithuania and my expectations and hopes for that. John was still very much aware that my life would be taking me away soon, and as we looked at each other we knew our time was short. He asked if I would be back to see him before I left for Lithuania—I told him I would not. He wished me well on my journey. Looking at him, it occurred to me that he, too, was preparing for his own departure. I said, "You know, John, it looks like we both have quite a journey ahead of us." "Yes, we do," he said, "yes, we do," with a slight tilt back of the head and a mystical look upward and away—his characteristic posture when he would articulate some great insight.

A short while later I got up to say goodbye to Pat and the other family members there. Pat and I embraced, and I bid her peace and promised I'd pray for them all. I then sat down again next to John, and, putting my hand on his, blessed him and bid him a good journey.

On 26 August 2004, eleven days after I had completed the first stage of my journey, John departed on the final stage of his journey. Now, as I stood there on the beach, facing westward over the Baltic Sea toward John's native Ireland, I spoke upon the wind the words of Yeats that John had requested his youngest daughter read that day at his memorial service. As I read aloud, I prayed silently that God had granted John the peace he sought:

The Valley of Shadows

> I will arise and go now, and go to Innisfree ...
> And I shall have some peace there, for peace comes dropping slow ...[4]

---

[4]. William Butler Yeats, "The Lake Isle of Innisfree."

6

Like Silent Human Sorrow—
A Disciple's Pondering

*I think of God, I am restless,
I ponder, and my spirit faints.*

—Psalm 77:3 (Book of Common Prayer)

*He was despised and rejected by people,
one who experienced pain and was acquainted with illness;
people hid their faces from him,
he was despised, and we considered him insignificant.
But he lifted up our illnesses, he carried our pain;
even though we thought he was being punished,
attacked by God, and afflicted for something he had done.
He was wounded because of our rebellious deeds;
crushed because of our sins;
he endured punishment that made us well;
because of his wounds we have been healed.*

—Isaiah 53:3–5 (NET)

The Valley of Shadows

> *That which he has not assumed has not been healed;*
> *but that which is united to his Godhead is also saved.*
>
> —Gregory of Nazianzus (4th c.)[1]

I wrote this reflection during my international service assignment at Lithuania Christian College in 2004–2005, while teaching a course in philosophy of religion, the central topic of which was the problem of evil. I had asked my students, drawn mostly from countries that had suffered under the Soviet Union, to develop their own philosophical-theological views on suffering and felt compelled to articulate my own view as well.

For several years prior to this, I had adopted a Lenten discipline of reading survivor memoirs and other first-hand accounts of the Holocaust. I read the remembrances and reflections of Elie Wiesel, Primo Levi, Saul Friedlander, Etty Hillesum, and others. This spiritual discipline was a contemporary counterpart to the church's ancient practice of recounting the story of the exodus, God's liberation of Israel from slavery in Egypt, as a preparation for remembering the story of the cross and resurrection, God's redemption of Jesus from death on behalf of all humanity. In effect, I had the sense that, to honestly celebrate the joy of resurrection on Easter Sunday, one had first to fully confront the acute suffering of the world—condensed into the agony of the cross—on Good Friday. But the agony of the cross, those Holocaust memoirs forced me to consider, was anything but past—innocent suffering was a present reality and not simply an abstract problem. This led me to ponder the suffering of innocents in the salvation of God—and thus the suffering of Jesus in the shadow of the horror of the Holocaust. Can we confess the cross of Christ as the salvation of a world plagued by the memory of Auschwitz?

The cross, it seemed to me, presented a starting point for speaking about both God and evil. At the cross, God did not explain to us that evil is necessary for the divine purpose or that innocent suffering is made good in a higher harmony (two common types of "theodicy," believed by even sincere Christians). Instead, God-in-Christ acted for us by interposing himself amidst the world's evil and personally taking upon himself all the sin and suffering of the world. At this point, without my realizing it, my thinking began to follow the pattern of the Eastern theologian of the ancient church, Gregory of Nazianzus. Gregory's formula "the unassumed is the unhealed" expresses his conviction

---

1. Quoted from Gregory of Nazianzus, *On God and Man*, 2.

that the Incarnation of God—hence, both the full humanity and full deity of Christ—is essential to an adequate Christian doctrine of salvation: Christ, God the Son incarnate, heals humanity of its sin-induced corruption-unto-death by "assuming" our full nature (body and soul) unto himself and uniting it to his Godhead. I came to a parallel view, that the Incarnation is essential to an adequate Christian theodicy: God personally confronts evil, and at the same time succors humanity in its suffering, by "assuming" unto himself and thus making his own both the sins and the sufferings of humanity through the full humanity and full deity—the life, death, and resurrection—of Christ.

~

Why do the righteous suffer? Why do the wicked prosper? This was Job's question. This was Asaph's dilemma (Ps 73). This was Jeremiah's lament (Jer 12:1–4). This is the perennial human question. It is the most mysterious of theological questions; for it calls into question all that tradition has taught about God: How can a world full of evil—suffering and pain, cruelty and injustice—be the creation of an all-powerful, all-loving God? It is also the thorniest of moral questions; for innocent suffering overturns our common ideas about justice: If God allows the innocent to suffer, what is the point of our being righteous and doing justice? Can a world in which the innocent suffer and the wicked prosper be ordered and governed by a just God? Yet, beneath and beyond theological problems and moral reasoning lie the existential questions of faith: Can we continue to entrust our lives and futures to a God who would allow the innocent to suffer? Can I accept salvation, if it requires the suffering of even one innocent victim?

In the patristic period, Augustine articulated the paradigm that has guided Christian thinking down the centuries concerning the meaning of suffering and the justification of God in a world created and sustained by God yet plagued and besieged by evil. According to Augustine, evil enters creation not by divinely preordained plan; for God is Creator of all, and God creates all things good. Rather, evil enters by way of creaturely sin: evil is the result of the Fall—creatures willfully turning away from God and God's purposes, from love of God to love of self. Humans sin when they freely use what God has created good for purposes contrary to God's will. In his perfect foreknowledge, God foresaw that his creatures would sin; yet

The Valley of Shadows

God also "foresaw the good which He Himself would bring out of [man's] evil."[2]

While Augustine's diagnosis of the origin and nature of evil follows standard patristic theology, his particular interpretation of the ultimate significance of suffering—his theodicy—is problematic. On Augustinian terms, pain and suffering is deserved punishment from God for sin and effects correction of the sinner's will. Suffering on earth also teaches us to anticipate happiness in heaven rather than place our hope in things on earth. All pain and suffering, in Augustine's view, is thus right (just retribution for sin) or good (didactic and salvific, contributing toward the eternal life of the soul). Augustinian theodicy is exemplified by the sermon of Father Paneloux to the plague-stricken people of the Algerian coastal town of Oran in Albert Camus' novel, *The Plague*:

> Calamity has come on you, my brethren, and my brethren, you deserved it . . . The just man need have no fear, but the evildoer has good cause to tremble. For plague is the flail of God . . . And thus, my brothers, at last it is revealed to you, the divine compassion which has ordained good and evil in everything; wrath and pity; the plague and your salvation. This same pestilence which is slaying you works for your good and points your path . . . It reveals the will of God in action, unfailingly transforming evil into good.[3]

Augustinian theodicy thus resolves the question of God and suffering by denying that there is any innocent suffering—all suffering is justified and necessary, deserved as punishment for sin (if not willful sin, then "original sin") or effective unto salvation.

Naïve confidence in Augustinian theodicy is no longer possible after Auschwitz. Instead of Augustinian thinking, my path of reflection through "the valley of the shadow of death" follows the way suggested by Kenneth Surin, the way of the cross:

> The Christian who takes the atonement seriously has no real need for theodicy . . . What God reveals is that divinity itself, through the cross of the Son, endures the sufferings that afflict us . . . The revelation that constitutes the core of "theodicy" . . . is, and can only be, God's action to bring salvation to humankind in and through the life, death and resurrection of Jesus Christ. The Christian "answer" to the "problem of evil" is the hesitant, stammering

2. Augustine, *City of God*, quoted from Peterson, *Problem of Evil*, 191.
3. Camus, *Plague*, 89, 90, 93.

bringing of this reconciling action to speech. This, one hopes, is the only approach to the "problem of evil" that can even aspire to reflect the true dimensions of the epistemological crises, and the spiritual predicaments, of the Ivan Karamazovs of this world . . .[4]

Before Auschwitz . . . there was Ivan Karamazov, Dostoevsky's infamous rebel against faith. Ivan describes to his younger brother Alyosha, a novice monk, horrifying stories of innocent children cruelly tortured and brutally murdered. He then presses the question of tragedy and justice to its logical limits:[5]

> *I want to see with my own eyes the lamb lie down with the lion and the resurrected victim rise and embrace his murderer. I want to be here when everyone understands why the world has been arranged the way it is. It is on that craving for understanding that all human religions are founded, so I am a believer. But then, what about the children? How will we ever account for their sufferings? . . . Listen, even if we assume that every person must suffer because his suffering is necessary to pay for eternal harmony, still do tell me, for God's sake, where the children come in. I can understand the concept of solidarity in sin and also solidarity in retribution. But how can there be solidarity in sin with small children? . . . And while there is still time, I want to dissociate myself from it all; I have no wish to be part of their eternal harmony. It's not worth one single tear of the martyred little girl who beat her breast with her tiny fist, shedding her innocent tears and praying to "sweet Jesus" to rescue her in the stinking outhouse. It's not worth it because that tear will have remained unatoned for. And those tears must be atoned for; otherwise there can be no harmony. But who could atone for those tears? How is it possible to atone for them?*

Ivan realizes
    that atonement for the innocent victim is impossible,
    that that single tear of that little girl remains unatoned for,
        unless the merciless logic of retributive justice
            can be decisively broken:
                the price of atonement is the sacrifice of forgiveness.
But *who*, he asks, has the *right* to forgive?

---

4. Surin, "Taking Suffering Seriously," 339–40 (emphasis added). Astonishingly, the cross of Christ not only is not the center of, but is peripheral to, Augustinian theodicy.

5. Quotations (in italics) from Dostoevsky, *Brothers Karamazov*, 294–96.

The Valley of Shadows

        Only the victim, he answers himself:
              unless the victim embraces her murderer
        there can be no "harmony."
    But the victim is dead.
So, again, he asks, is this possible?
    Is there one single creature in the whole world
    who could forgive or would have the right to do so?
Possessed by his own insatiable demand for vengeance—
    I still need retribution.
    Without it I'd rather destroy myself.
    And I must have that retribution
    not somewhere far off in infinity
    but here, on earth.—
Ivan rejects salvation by atonement at the price of forgiveness:

> *No, I want no part of any harmony; I don't want it out of love for mankind. I prefer to remain with my unavenged suffering and my unappeased anger*—even if I happen to be wrong. . . . *such harmony is rather overpriced.*

He thus concludes with a challenge to Alyosha:

> *Tell me yourself—I challenge you: let's assume that you were called upon to build the edifice of human destiny so that men would finally be happy and would find peace and tranquility. If you knew that, in order to attain this, you would have to torture just one single creature, let's say the little girl . . . and that on her unavenged tears you could build that edifice, would you agree to it? Tell me and don't lie!*

Alyosha replies quietly:
    No, I would not.

The Christian gospel,
    the good news of God spoken in flesh through Jesus Christ,
dares answer Ivan's questions
    Is atonement possible?
    Is there one single creature in the whole world
    who could forgive or would have the right to do so?
with a bold *Yes!*—God!
    This is the scandalous wisdom of the gospel:
    God's kingdom of justice is revealed
    and God's promise of salvation is fulfilled

through the suffering, dying, and rising
of that most innocent of all—Jesus, God-incarnate.
> Through the cross and resurrection of Jesus,
> God embraces us, his murderers—
>> murdering hostility, overcoming alienation,
>> offering forgiveness, demonstrating love,
>> speaking peace, making atonement,
>> reconciling us to himself, creating us anew—
> thus liberating humanity, and justice, from captivity to both sin
> and the law of retribution that demands death
>> as satisfaction for sin
>> (Luke 23–24; John 20–21; Rom 5; 2 Cor 5; Eph 2).

Ironically, the gospel confirms Ivan's rebellion—
not even fulfillment of God's plan of salvation,
not even consummation of God's kingdom,
is worth the unatoned tears of a single child:
> the gospel renounces a global economy of good and evil
>> that balances evil and good as costs and benefits;
> the gospel renounces an eschatological calculus
>> of suffering and glory
>> that justifies infliction of cruelty and injustice upon some
>> as necessary for the ultimate enjoyment of peace by others,
>> that accounts the victims of the system
>> within a margin of acceptable loss
>> for the sake of the final good.

Every tear, *each* wound
must be atoned for, healed,
must be suffered, assumed by God-in-Christ,
incorporated into the identity of the Incarnate One,
poured into the healing wounds of the Suffering Servant-Son,
through the life, death, and resurrection of Jesus—
> "He took our infirmities and bore our diseases" (Matt 8:17),
> "By his wounds [we] have been healed" (1 Pet 2:24)—

or else God's kingdom is aborted,
God's salvation stillborn.
We may, then, with Alyosha quietly refuse our consent
to justify the innocent suffering of a single victim
in the name of any "higher harmony."

The Valley of Shadows

> The Seer has seen and testified
> that through the cross and resurrection of Jesus Christ
> the tears of the victims on earth are vindicated
> and the cries of the martyrs in heaven are answered;
>> for the Lamb that was slaughtered
>> is worthy to receive
>> blessing and honor and glory and power
>> forever and ever. Amen. (Rev 4–7)

But can there be "Amen" after Auschwitz?

Having grown up in an Hasidic Jewish community,
Elie Wiesel found himself at not quite fifteen years old
disembarking a train at Auschwitz,
separated forever from his mother and sister
by eight words:[6]
> *Men to the left! Women to the right!*

As he stood in line beside his father,
uncertain of their fate—
> to the prison camp or to the crematory—

someone began to recite the Kaddish,
the traditional Jewish prayer for the dead:
> *May his Name be blessed and magnified . . .*

His father joined in the prayer.
At that moment, Elie's heart rose up in rebellion:

> *Why should I bless His name? The Eternal, Lord of the Universe, the All-Powerful and Terrible, was silent. What had I to thank him for?*

Their line then marched toward
an inferno-filled ditch
into which a lorry had just dumped
a load of little children, babies.
Would that be their fate as well?
Elie deliberated throwing himself against the electric fence
rather than being thrown into the burning pit.
Despite the revolt of his heart,
he heard the words pass over his own lips
> *May His Name be blessed and magnified . . .*

---

6. Quotations (in italics) from Wiesel, *Night*, 27, 31, 32, 61–62.

Like Silent Human Sorrow—A Disciple's Pondering

as he faced into death and the line turned
and they marched past the pit into the barracks.

> *Never shall I forget that night, the first night in the camp, which has turned my life into one long night, seven times cursed and seven times sealed. . . .*
>
> *Never shall I forget those flames which consumed my faith forever.*
>
> *Never shall I forget that nocturnal silence which deprived me, for all eternity, of the desire to live. Never shall I forget those moments which murdered my God and my soul and turned my dreams to dust. Never shall I forget these things, even if I am condemned to live as long as God Himself. Never.*

Wiesel recounts how one evening,
after another day of forced labor in the factory,
the company of prisoners was compelled to witness
the hanging of three prisoners on charges of sabotage:

> *One day when we came back from work, we saw three gallows rearing up in the assembly place, three black crows . . . Three victims in chains—and one of them, the little servant, the sad-eyed angel. . . .*
>
> *All eyes were on the child. He was lividly pale, almost calm, biting his lips. The gallows threw its shadow over him. . . .*
>
> *"Long live liberty!" cried the two adults.*
>
> *But the child was silent.*
>
> *"Where is God? Where is He?" someone behind me asked.*
>
> *At a sign from the head of the camp, the three chairs tipped over.*
>
> *Total silence throughout the camp. On the horizon, the sun was setting. . . .*
>
> *Then the march past began. The two adults were no longer alive. . . . But the third rope was still moving; being so light, the child was still alive. . . .*
>
> *For more than half an hour he stayed there, struggling between life and death, dying in slow agony under our eyes. And we had to look him full in the face. . . .*
>
> *Behind me, I heard the same man asking:*
>
> *"Where is God now?"*

The Valley of Shadows

> *And I heard a voice within me answer him:*
>
> *"Where is He? Here He is—He is hanging here on this gallows..."*

After Auschwitz...
    where babies burn in ditches, children hang from gallows,
    and the ominous silence of heaven
    transfigures into the immense absence of God—
the only God who can withstand trial by accusation
in the presence of the innocent victims,
the only God who can live to see dawning light
beyond the abyss of infernal night—
    the night of burning bodies and billowing ash,
    the night of murdered souls and consumed faith—
        is the sorrow-filled God
            who tastes upon his own lips
            and drinks into eternal memory
            each tear wept by every victim,
            who hears in his own ears
            and cradles with eternal care
            the bitter silence of anguished agony
            that had long-since ceased to sound
            from the life-drained bodies hanging upon the gallows,
    the broken-hearted, broken-bodied God
        who joins himself to the world
        at the very place
        where the world is disjointed
        that he might reunite a broken world
        by uniting the world to himself,
        who binds his being to humanity
        with the sinews of suffering and sacrifice
        that he might heal us of our wound
        by assuming our affliction into himself
        and making our woe his own.

The only God whose goodness and justice are worthy of our thanks and
    praise,
the only God whose Name we dare bless aloud—
    in the face of unspeakable evil,
    in the shadow of the gallows—

Like Silent Human Sorrow—A Disciple's Pondering

  is the God who became human flesh and blood,
    who surrenders power to redeem his creation
      and wills vulnerability to violence by his creatures,
    who realizes freedom among the slaves
      and chooses solidarity alongside the victims,
    who suffers passionately with us and for us
      and dies defenselessly as one of us to save us,
    who hangs in weakness upon the gallows
      and swallows death in victory from the grave—
      only to arise with head, hands, feet, and side
      still marked with visible wounds (John 20:24–29).

Not the Geometric Deity of Aristotle,
  existing abstractly, apathetically in Absolute Being,
  like an Ideal Euclidean figure—
    a Circular Contemplative turning perpetually upon itself.
  That is the God about which the wicked boast in the pride of their countenance,
  the God in which the wicked believe in the thoughts of their hearts,
  the God that does not call mortals to account for their wicked deeds (Ps 10)—
    the God that has forgotten the world,
    the God that has buried his face in the bosom of his own being,
    the God that will never see the suffering of the weak
      and helpless,
    much less seek out justice for the oppressed.

Nor the Cosmic Deity of the Stoics,
  the Providence that governs the cosmos by the inexorable
    Law of Nature,
 saying:
    Learn to want what you get.
    That disease is actually for your health.
    This torture works for your own good in the end.
      Your child is dead,
      but it's all for the best—
      God has a plan for your pain.
    All human suffering works the divine will.
    Whatever evil you see here is compensated by good elsewhere.

The Valley of Shadows

> All things, good and evil, contribute to the cosmic harmony.

If compassion—co-suffering—
    does not flood the bowels of God;
if God does not, truly and really,
    bear our afflictions and infirmities,
    with us and for us (Isa 53:4–5);
if God does not risk suffering
    our diseases and tortures,
    much less sacrifice himself
    to liberate us from our suffering (1 Pet 2:19–24);
if divine compassion does not involve God,
    personally and painfully,
    in the redemption of the cosmos from the dominion
    of sin and death (Rom 8);
if, instead, divine compassion is only
    a pious sentiment, a righteous wish
    that creation would someday be freed of its travail:
        then God is a fraud—
        not worth his word,
        not worth our trust.

Not those false gods,
but the only true God:

The God who enters the world
where the angel of cruelty and suffering
has barred "the way to love"
and joins himself to the world of human agony and suffering,
so that, though God is "king of time,"
"Time is the canvas stretched by [God's] pain."[7]

The God who is:
    the Faithful Father revealed in history to our ancestors
        who hears the groaning and observes the misery of his people,
        knows our sufferings and remembers his promises,
        and comes down to deliver us so that we might worship him
        (Exod 2:23—3:12);

---

7. Rilke, *Book of Hours*, I, 53.

Like Silent Human Sorrow—A Disciple's Pondering

    the Living Spirit who spoke through prophets of old
        and now dwells within us,
        sharing our pains and voicing our sighs,
        bringing our suffering into God's presence (Rom 8:9–27);
    the Pensive Christ hymned in poet's verse—
        our watchful Lord keeping vigil "like silent human sorrow"
        by the roadside where he can see
        "only our woes pass by with heavy sighs."[8]

Still . . .
If Christ is *not* raised from the dead,
    then God was tried, convicted, hanged, and incinerated in Auschwitz
    and our faith is in vain.
But if Christ *is* raised from the dead,
    then not even Auschwitz can condemn God
    and our faith may yet be a living hope.

Because, and only because, God speaks his *Yes* in Jesus (2 Cor 1:20)
    through even innocent suffering and shameful death,
and because, and only because, God's spoken *Yes* in Jesus
    is not forever silenced by trial and crucifixion
    but is vindicated by resurrection and exaltation,
        God, and we in God's name, may speak *Yes*
        to that awful, unvoiced utterance in the midst of Auschwitz:
            Where is God? Here He is—
            He is hanging here on this gallows.

Because, and only because, God has borne the evil of death
    in his body-self, Jesus,
    and yet offered his executioners mercy (Luke 23:34),
        God, and we in God's name, may forgive the unforgivable,
        and so speak *Yes* to Ivan's tormenting questions:
            Is atonement possible?
            Is there one single creature in the whole world
            who could forgive or would have the right to do so?

Because, and only because, God speaks his *Yes* in Jesus

---

8. Mykolaitis-Putinas, "Pensive Christ by the Roadside." This poem refers to a wood-carved "Man of Sorrows" (*Rupintojelis*), a traditional depiction of Christ in Lithuanian Catholic folk spirituality. One finds such carvings across the Lithuanian countryside.

The Valley of Shadows

>   through human, humble, obedient service,
>   even to the point of suffering and death,
> because, and only because, God exalts the crucified Jesus above all,
>   may our knee bend
>   and our tongue confess
>   "Jesus Christ is Lord"
>   to the glory of God (Phil 2:5–11).

The Way of Life

*"I came that they may have life,
and have it abundantly."*

—John 10:10

*"I am the way,
and the truth,
and the life."*

—John 14:6

*There are two Ways:
a Way of Life and a Way of Death,
and the difference between these two Ways is great.*

—The Didache 1.1[1]

---

1. *Early Christian Writings*, 191.

7

What We Live By—
A Disciple's Daily Bread

Ho, everyone who thirsts, come to the waters;
and you that have no money, come, buy and eat!
Come, buy wine and milk without money and without price.
Why do you spend your money for that which is not bread,
and your labor for that which does not satisfy?
Listen carefully to me, and eat what is good,
and delight yourselves in rich food.
Incline your ear, and come to me;
listen, so that you may live.

—Isaiah 55:1-3a

About a year after I had made a whole-life commitment to follow Jesus, in the spring of 2000, I was presented with an offer I could not refuse but almost did. On two separate occasions, fellow congregation members suggested that I should consider becoming the next leader of Jeremiah House, a Service Adventure unit of Mennonite Mission Network that was supported by our congregation, Kern Road Mennonite Church, in South Bend, Indiana. At first I was hesitant: voluntary service is a fine thing, I thought, but did I want to become entangled in the messiness of community life? After the second prompting, however, I knew that the Holy Spirit was at work in the words of my sister and brother. I realized that I needed to pray about this, and following a time of discernment I said "yes"—which proved to be a pivotal "yes" in my life in unexpected ways.

I had never before lived in, much less been the leader of, an intentional Christian community. It was a steep learning curve—a difficult challenge, to say the least, but a grace-filled process, as I would eventually discover. Indeed, it was through this experience that I came to understand personally that the true substance of life, the real stuff of abundant life, is nothing other than grace. Throughout my time as house leader, I relied for counsel on that time-tested guide for Christian community, the Rule of Saint Benedict, whose wisdom nurtured in my heart and mind a sense and vision for Christian life suffused in grace.

The following piece draws from two sources: a worship presentation at Kern Road Mennonite Church, in June 2002, and a public presentation on the occasion of Martin Luther King, Jr. Day, in January 2004, at a workshop to promote a new Youth Justice Project as an alternative to the juvenile justice system.[1]

We Live by Grace

"We live by gifts, not by what we earn." So did Garrison Keillor, renowned storyteller and folk theologian, sum up "the news from Lake Wobegon" one Saturday evening on his radio program, *A Prairie Home Companion*. When I'd realized what he'd said, I sat stunned for a moment at what I'd heard; for it occurred to me that I could not think of a simpler way to summarize the gospel, the good news of God's grace. It reminds me of the message proclaimed by the prophet, who invites us to feast freely on the riches of God's goodness, to satisfy our souls with abundant bread from heaven, the bread that gives life. The source and sustenance of our life is not in us, our own efforts or merits or entitlements, but rather in what we undeservedly and unexpectedly receive from and give to others—and, ultimately, God. After

---

1. For further reflections on Christian community and voluntary service based on my experience in Service Adventure, see my essay, "Service and Sacrifice."

securing all our individual gains, after counting all our personal successes, we are still needy, if only because we can neither manufacture nor earn for ourselves one essential thing—love. Thus the prophet asks us: Why expend yourself on what does not satisfy your soul, much less give you life?

After proclaiming the good news of the resurrection of Christ and confessing his own inadequacy to be called an apostle, the Apostle Paul declares that, nonetheless, grace is the substance of his being, the means of his existence: "But by the grace of God I am what I am, and his grace toward me has not been in vain" (1 Cor 15:10). According to Paul, the primary giver and sustainer of life is Christ; and we live in Christ by freely receiving his love in faith, so that we who live by faith in the love of Christ no longer live on the merit of our own effort: "It is no longer I who live, but it is Christ who lives in me. And the life I now live in the flesh I live by faith in the Son of God, who loved me and gave himself for me" (Gal 2:20). The grace by which I live is not the Reformation theological abstraction whereby guilt inherited through original sin is cancelled in a legal transaction between God the Father and God the Son at the cross, a satisfaction of God that leaves me, this person in the flesh, substantially unchanged. Paul said otherwise—grace is precisely that reality whereby God-in-Christ lives in me in the flesh. Day by day, as I freely receive the love of Christ in faith, I am being personally transformed so that Christ is really present in me and sustains my every breath. Paul speaks of this transformation as a radical renewal of creation: "If anyone is in Christ, there is a new creation: everything old has passed away; see, everything has become new" (2 Cor 5:17)! Furthermore, Christ did not die so that I might live for myself alone. That I live by faith in the love of Christ—indeed, that the crucified and risen Christ lives in and through me—entails that I must now live for Christ: "For the love of Christ urges us on … [Christ] died for all, so that those who live might live no longer for themselves, but for him who died and was raised for them" (2 Cor 5:14–15).

This life of transforming grace is not for me to live in isolation, however—it is not just me and Jesus. For to live by grace one must freely receive, and give, love in faith; and that implies being in relationship with others. We live by faith when we see the face of Christ, the image of God, in each other and, seeing Christ present in each other, either respond with mercy to the need of the other or in humility allow the other to serve one's own need. The need of the other is God's invitation to fellowship, and the gift of the other is God's offer of blessing. It is thus by life together in a community of grace—this merciful offering and humble receiving of love—that one lives fully in Christ. Community is *sacrament*, a truly living, visible sign to the world of God's grace made manifest in the flesh. It is a corporate *we* that concretely embodies Christ in the world.

We Live by Faith

From 2000 to 2004 I lived in community with several young adults as leader of a voluntary service unit. By partaking of the life of this community, I came to taste and see the incarnate grace of which Keillor and Paul speak. There was manna enough for us day by day as together we endeavored by the grace of God and the power of the Holy Spirit to live simply; share routine responsibilities; be accountable to one another for resources, time, and behavior; worship God together in spirit and in truth; live out our words; bear with one another's burdens and limitations; affirm each other's gifts; listen to the message of wisdom spoken by the other; receive guests with generous hospitality; and "seek the *shalom* of the city" (Jer 29:7, our mission statement) by being instruments of peace in service to both neighbors and strangers in need.

Although we lived together in a voluntary *service* unit, I came to realize that service was not primarily what we were about. Instead, I believe, the primary social task of our unit was to be a household of faith. If we did not witness faithfully to the *shalom* of God's kingdom by our very being-together, then how could we effectively seek the *shalom* of our city for God? After all, as Alan Kreider has observed, when it comes to alternative models of social living, "The church has nothing to offer the world other than what it has learned to live in its own domestic life."[2]

What communal discipleship teaches are those spiritual disciplines of personal sacrifice (of privacy, autonomy, self-gratification, and self-sufficiency) that are necessary for cultivating the virtues of character (humility, patience, compassion, gratitude, and generosity), which are themselves necessary for implementing the practices of community (mutual accountability, sharing resources, bearing burdens, and forgiving grievances) by which human lives of Christ-like service are possible and sustainable (cf. Eph 4:17—5:2; Phil 2:1–13; Col 3:1–17). Community teaches us the virtue of moderating individual desire with concern for the common good by using our freedom to serve the well-being of one another: "For you were

---

2. Kreider et al., *Culture of Peace*, 61.

What We Live By—A Disciple's Daily Bread

called to freedom, brothers and sisters; only do not use your freedom as an opportunity for self-indulgence, but through love become slaves to one another" (Gal 5:13). Most importantly, community invites us into mutual vulnerability, to need and value one another as equal members of one body (1 Cor 12:12–27).

We were, in a very real sense, a "household of God" being "built together spiritually into a dwelling place for God" (Eph 2:19–22). Over those years I had the awesome privilege of entering the "Holy of Holies" in the most ordinary of circumstances because my community members incarnated God for me, and I for them, in many ways. In our midst, God came near as we . . . danced for joy and sang with praise and thanksgiving; played guitar, piano, and didjeridoo; laughed aloud and cried in silence; listened attentively as we told stories of struggle and success, prayed about hopes and fears, and mused on future plans; showed us a wounded heart and welcomed our embrace; prepared food in our kitchen and shared tea at our table of plenty.

Now, for sure, we were far from perfect. In actuality, we sometimes failed to "maintain the unity of the Spirit in the bond of peace" (Eph 4:3). And in the daily rub of things our garments of "compassion, kindness, humility, meekness, and patience" (Col 3:12) often wore thin. That is why the "ministry of reconciliation" (2 Cor 5:18) is an essential practice in the discipleship community. This means that the cross—by which former enemies make peace with one another, and, having been made friends in Christ, together enjoy peace with God (Rom 5:6ff; Eph 2:11ff.)—is the necessary center of life together in Christ. Christian community, then, is a pilgrimage of peacemaking, an ongoing process of patching holes and mending tears where the garment of love has worn too thin (Col 3:14).

This life of grace is hard work requiring intentionality, for the yoke of community does not come naturally to us. What community is about is radically countercultural; and each of us has, more or less, passively imbibed from the secular milieu an individualistic ethos that idolizes the autonomous, sufficient self and portrays accountability and interdependence as weakness and deficiency. Each of us is thus in need of daily conversion to community. Community calls us to contract the self to make room for the other and reminds us that before the other we stand on holy ground. Especially in the presence of the other's weakness—which cries out to us, "Help me, have mercy"—we are called to put off our shoes of pride and power and approach with "the fear of the Lord" instead of wielding our rights in self-vindication. Acutely aware of our own moral frailty and the fragility of our life together, we must offer and receive forgiveness, time and time again.

Grace is precisely that by which it is possible for competing and conflicting individuals to live together as a "we" in a communion of peace: we live by grace—or the "we" dies.

We Live by Peace

As a Christian household community, we lived by a covenant that both set boundaries on acceptable behavior as well as committed us to dealing with transgression of community boundaries in a way that seeks to heal rather than hurt, a way that seeks to correct wrongdoers rather than inflicting painful penalties to punish wrongdoing, a way that seeks to right relationships that have been ruptured and restore the brother or sister who has strayed from the path of right rather than to subject him or her to judgment and rejection. In this we aimed to follow the scriptural instruction of the Apostle Paul:

> My friends, if anyone is detected in a transgression, you who have received the Spirit should restore such a one in a spirit of gentleness. Take care that you yourselves are not tempted. Bear one another's burdens, and in this way you will fulfill the law of Christ. (Gal 6:1–2)

In one situation during my four years as Servant Adventure leader, I found myself needing to deal with some serious wrongdoing—a member of our household had transgressed nearly every major community boundary, transgressions that were clearly grounds for dismissal from our community, including: habitual lying/deception; drug, alcohol, and tobacco use; failing other house members; and being late to work. His transgressions also involved his roommate in concealing his wrongdoing. This was serious stuff that I, as house leader, could not take lightly—the trust and fidelity that are fundamental to community life had been violated and the basic integrity of our household was at stake. For sure, he had to be held accountable and could not be permitted to continue in his wrongdoing. At the same time, simply dismissing him from the community would have resolved nothing: the wrongs he had done would not have been set right, relationships that had been broken would not have been healed, and rather than restoring our community we would instead have been dismembered. The way to deal with such wrongdoing according to retributive justice would have been to throw the book at him—to deal out the painful consequences of his behavior, to impose on him the penalty he had coming, to give him just deserts. But then there would have been no forgiveness, no reconciliation, no healing of hurt, no freedom of release for either him or our household from the wrong that had been done—no grace, no atonement, no peace.

Once his transgressions were uncovered, I resolved that we would deal with him as the scripture instructs—restore him with gentleness. We dealt with his wrongdoing through a disciplinary process: (a) He had to confess fully his transgressions in front of the entire household and face everyone's reaction, hear other house members express the hurt and anger of damaged trust. (b) He had to hear me as house leader pronounce judgment that by his transgression he had broken faith with us; it was now up to him whether he would choose to remain part of our community by taking steps to make things right and so make good our claim of him as a brother. (c) He had to promise to walk the right way from then on and agree to measures of accountability that restricted his freedom away from the house and permitted us to hold him to his promises—if he failed at this, he would be asked to leave our community.

This disciplinary process proved far more successful than I had anticipated: he never again offended during the rest of his year with us; but even more importantly, he learned that our trust was important to him *and* that he mattered to us. Now, all was not thereby perfect—restorative discipline is no magic wand that makes it as if the wrongdoing and the hurt didn't happen. It was hard for some house members to fully trust him again, and a residue of resentment against him did remain. So, although there was reconciliation in that he was restored to membership as one of us, there was still resistance by some to full relationship, a resistance he was aware of even though it was unspoken. This, though, taught him a further lesson—having to go on living with those whom he had offended but who had received him back into fellowship taught him that trust is fragile and that breaking trust creates deep hurt and lasting effects. Had we dismissed him from the community as punishment for his wrongdoing, he would never have had to face the real consequences of his actions and take responsibility for the harm he had caused.[3]

---

3. This episode is an example of what is called "restorative justice." For an excellent exposition of the biblical theology of restorative justice, see Marshall, *Beyond Retribution*,

The Way of Life

We Live by Thanks

Reflecting on my role as community leader (especially my own failures to be gracious), I have drawn three practical lessons:

- As others change, be open to change in yourself. Let others surprise you, and let yourself surprise you. For the Spirit moves beyond your categories, labels, and judgments.

- Rules are necessary for accountability, but relationships are more important than rules. The rules we make are always arbitrary to some degree, but we cannot live without relationships. While a rule should not be broken simply to avoid bending a relationship (sometimes we do need to repent, to "turn around"), bend a rule before breaking a relationship. When a wrong requires righting to save the integrity of the community, justice should be redemptive, not punitive, allowing possibility for repentance, reconciliation, and renewal.

- Receive each person as a gift from God, and treat each one as you would God's most precious gift, Jesus Christ. When (not if!) you fall short of that, confess your sin to God and each other. Be forgiven. And forgive. For it is grace that sustains the relationships necessary for life and which gives freedom to change.

I don't pretend that I practiced servant leadership perfectly in the Service Adventure unit. Indeed, I still have much to learn, and my housemates were some of my best teachers. That was a principal motivation for deciding to extend my initial two-year term of service for a second term as leader of Jeremiah House. At one point I had thought that if the second year of my first term were a good year I would take it and exit, feeling satisfied for having fulfilled my commitment. I had even started looking forward to a future in a land flowing with milk and honey. As I remembered how much God had provided for me thus far, however, I realized that I was forgetting how much I needed the manna of my community. Cognizant of my own ingratitude, I mused: had Israel been satisfied with and thankful for manna from heaven, they could have lived and worshipped God in the desert forever. The promised land is where God feeds us today and we give thanks for our daily bread.

Upon announcing over dinner my decision to serve another term, one of my housemates asked the very question that had concerned me, "Aren't

---

as well as my own book, *Atonement, Justice, and Peace*.

you worried that next year might be worse?" My reply was straightforward: While it is a law of nature that things could always be worse, in the most important respect next year will be the same as this year and the year before—a gift from God.

8

For God So Loved the World—
A Disciple's Witness

> *I call heaven and earth to witness against you today
> that I have set before you
> life and death, blessings and curses.
> Choose life so that you and your descendants may live...*
>
> —Deuteronomy 30:19

> *For God so loved the world that he gave his only Son,
> so that everyone who believes in him
> may not perish but may have eternal life.
> Indeed, God did not send the Son into the world to condemn the world,
> but in order that the world might be saved through him.*
>
> —John 3:16–17

In 1999 one of the pastors of my congregation at the time issued a challenge: a capital murder trial was to begin in our city, and he was inviting folks to join in a quiet public witness for life and peace—and against the death penalty—during the trial. I responded immediately, which would prove to be another pivotal "yes" in my life. For many years I had been opposed to the death penalty on account of the gospel: when Jesus said, "Let the one without sin cast the first stone" (John 8:7), I took that literally and concluded that humans had no right to execute the death penalty.[1] But I had never before given public witness to my faith conviction—and in the midst of the trial I would find myself testifying to my faith on the front page of the local newspaper. When the trial moved to the penalty phase, our quiet witness transformed into a vocal but prayerful and peaceful demonstration that drew a hundred participants from various denominations. That experience precipitated the formation of a local coalition of Christians—comprising Mennonites, Catholics, Brethren, Methodists, Baptists, Episcopalians, and others—that would witness for life and against the death penalty in our county over the next five years.[2]

In the meantime, while I organized the work of this Choose Life Coalition against the Death Penalty, I was approached by a prominent member of our congregation with a simple question: Witness against the death penalty was fine, he said, but what about abortion? Why were we not as actively and vocally opposed to abortion? His question brought the silence of our congregation—and our denomination—on the issue of abortion to my attention for the first time. I promised him that I would work to redress that deficiency and committed myself to think more carefully about it. Over the next several years I would write op-ed pieces in our denominational magazine, publish a scholarly article in a church-related academic journal, and make a presentation at our denominational national assembly to exhort the church to redress the inconsistencies in our witness for life and peace.[3]

The present reflection integrates my consistent pro-life/pro-peace convictions within an evangelical framework: God's "yes" to us in the life, death, and resurrection of Jesus, and our "yes" to God by faith in Jesus, have their practical correlate in our saying "yes" to the gift of life and "no" to the powers of death—abortion, capital punishment, and war.

The original version was proclaimed in worship at Prairie Street Mennonite Church (Elkhart, Indiana) in February 2006. Specific acts of prayer referred to near the end relate to actual events in the congregational life at

---

1. My subsequent studies would substantiate that early conviction. See my careful analysis of the incident of "the woman caught in adultery" in John 8 in my book, *Atonement, Justice, and Peace*, 474–88.

2. See Stoner, "Death Penalty."

3. See "Thinking clearly about abortion," "Thinking clearly about abortion, again," and "Toward a Consistent Ethic of Life."

Prairie Street. Portions are adapted from my essay, "Tragic zeal," published originally in The Mennonite *(2004).*[4]

~

A World Caught in a Death Spiral

We cannot forget the events of September 11, 2001—the horrific sight of the terrorist attacks, the collapse of the Twin Towers and the Pentagon in flames, in contrast with the heroic actions of firefighters, police officers, and ordinary folks. On that day we saw the stark contradiction between those willing to take their own lives in order to take the lives of others and those willing to risk their lives to save the lives of others. Commentators likened 9/11 to the attack on Pearl Harbor, calling it "a date that will live in infamy." And given that the war on terror subsequently ensnared the United States in a vicious cycle of violence and vengeance for thirteen years, such words may be prophetic in ways not originally intended.

Nearly two years after 9/11, the United States witnessed another date that should "live in infamy"—though it has received much less notice. On September 3, 2003, the State of Florida executed the anti-abortion activist and minister-turned-terrorist Paul Hill for the 1994 murder of an abortionist. This event showed us another glaring contradiction: secured behind prison walls, government officials strapped onto a table and fatally poisoned a man, a man who had been willing to gun down on the street another man using the same perverse logic—the killing of a defenseless person justified in the name of defending the innocent, defenseless lives of others. While there is much of which to be horrified in this event, there are no heroes to remember. For this event singularly reveals America's captivity to a death spiral of violence and vengeance.

        This death spiral took three turns.
        Some, for various reasons unknown to us,

---

[4] That essay was guided, in part, by this observation of Yoder, *He Came Preaching Peace*, 20: "No one created in God's image and for whom Christ died can be for me an enemy, whose life I am willing to threaten or to take, unless I am more devoted to something else—to a political theory, to a nation, to the defense of certain privileges, or to my own personal welfare—than I am to God's cause: his loving invasion of this world in his prophets, his Son, and his church."

The Way of Life

> sought to end certain problems by abortion;
> and another willingly and legally aided
> in killing the unborn
> in the name of freedom of choice.
> Yet another, taking the law into his own hands,
> sought to end abortion by killing the abortionist
> in the name of the sanctity of life.
> Finally, the state, whose laws do not protect equally
> the lives of the abortionist and the aborted,
> sought to end murder by killing the murderer
> in the name of "we the people."

This is the plot-line of a classical tragedy, played out in real life.[5]

We might be tempted to blame the tragic outcome of September 3, 2003 on one or the other of the major players. And in the days preceding and following Mr. Hill's execution, there were many opinions to be heard and read on the matter. The problem, some said, is that Mr. Hill's character was flawed by moral contradiction. The state's stubborn pursuit of the death penalty, others argued, succeeded only at making Hill into a martyr for his cause. The root of the problem, still others insisted, is the women seeking abortions and the abortionists performing them—or, others would rather emphasize, the extenuating circumstances that necessitate the choice of abortion in the first place. Each of these explanations may contain some truth, but together they miss the crucial point.

For each of the principal figures is zealously devoted to a political or moral cause that supposedly justifies violence, the deliberate destruction of life, if necessary: the abortionist is devoted to pro-choice, the activist-terrorist is devoted to pro-life, and the state is devoted to justice and security. Yet all of the actors are blinded by their zealotry to the image of God manifest in each human being. This zealous devotion prevents them from

---

5. Compare this real-life tragedy to that in Sophocles's classical Greek play, *Antigone*. Each of Sophocles's dramatic characters is zealously devoted to a cause that he or she believes is worthy of sacrificing life: Polyneices is devoted to seizing power, Creon to entrenching his authority, Antigone to her family and piety, Haemon to his betrothed, and Eurydice to her son. All the actors are blinded by their zeal from seeing wisdom, represented in the figure of the blind prophet Teiresias; and this bondage to passion prevents them from acting with prudence. And therein lies the tragedy. The consequence of collective blindness to wisdom and bondage to passion is a tragic sequence of events for Sophocles's players. Polyneices's act of treachery begets Creon's act of arrogance, which begets Antigone's act of defiance, which sets off a spiral of death: a death sentence is followed by suicide, which is followed by attempted murder and accidentally self-inflicted death, which is followed by another suicide.

seeing the others whom they would kill for the sake of their own cause as the very ones for whom Christ died, as those whom God so loved that he gave his only Son.

And herein lay the tragedy. Elevating their respective causes to ultimate value, each sees the life of another, not as a gift of God lovingly redeemed through the gift of the Son, but rather as a mere means that can be sacrificed to some other end. For the abortionist, the unborn is an obstacle to liberation; for the activist-terrorist, the abortionist is a threat to life; and for the state, the activist-terrorist is an offense against justice and a danger to security.

Consequently, a tragic cycle of violence and vengeance ensues, propelling the world further along its death spiral:
> the state takes the life of the activist-terrorist
> for taking the life of the abortionist
> for taking the life of the unborn.

The Gospel: "Choose life"

But now, this is the Good News:
> God sends the Son
> into this tragically hell-bent world,
> the very world that God created and loves,
> so that "the world might be saved through him" (John 3:17),
> so that we "may have life and have it abundantly" (10:10).[6]

And because we have known
God's love through the Son's life,
it is our calling as the church
to proclaim and live God's cause—
> God's loving invasion of this dying world
> to deliver it from darkness and destruction.

As God's people,
redeemed through the gift of God's own Son,
let us hear the same word
that Moses proclaimed to Israel—

---

6. All citations of scripture in this chapter are from the Gospel of John unless otherwise indicated.

The Way of Life

>the calling to "Choose life
>so that [we] and [our] descendants may live,
>loving the Lord [our] God, obeying him,
>and holding fast to him." (Deut 30:19–20)

Choosing life, we say
>*No* to every form of violence,
>*No* to every force of death
>>whether by individual choice
>>>or by state authority;
>>whether at the abortion clinic
>>>or on the streets
>>>or in our homes;
>>whether in the execution chamber
>>>or in the torture chamber
>>>or on the battlefield.

We say *No* to the way of violence and death
because God has spoken his *Yes*—
>a loving, saving, life-giving *Yes*
>to us through the Son—

and we have responded *Yes* to God.
And because we have said *Yes*
to God's loving cause
to redeem each and every life—
>indeed, to save the whole world—

we must speak an unequivocal *No*
to the utilitarian evaluation of human life:

>*No* to the view …
>>that converts human beings
>>>created in God's image and for God's purpose
>>>>into mere instruments for satisfying human desires;
>>that discounts the lives of some persons
>>>because they are judged "useless" by others;
>>that avers the rights of the vulnerable may be violated
>>>to satisfy the preferences of the privileged.

To those who have said *Yes* to God's love,
Jesus has given this commandment,

that we love one another as he has loved us (15:12).
The essential task of our Christian calling, therefore,
is to love others as God has loved us through the Son.

Now, if we are to love others as God has loved us,
then we must value the lives of others
with the same measure of love
by which God has redeemed our lives.
And the measure of God's love—
God's measure of the transcendent worth of human life—
is no less than the gift of God's own life through the Son:
> "For God so loved the world that he gave his only Son."

This, then, is the astonishing message of the gospel:
> that God loves and values each human life—
>> indeed, the whole world—
>
> as worth redeeming by no less than
> God's own life given through the Son
> for the life of the world (6:51).

Seen through God's saving love,
seen from God's redemptive cause,
we should regard all human lives—
indeed, all created things—
as worthy of love, as redeemable by God.

Imagine for a moment a flourishing adult human being.
Picture her in your mind's eye.
> Now, take away her professional competence,
> take away her financial security and social standing,
> take away her capacity to communicate and calculate,
> take away her ability to feed and clean herself,
> take away her power to move and breathe on her own,
> take away even her desire to continue living in such condition.

What remains in your imagination?
From the perspective of the gospel,
in this one essential respect,
what remains is the same as before:
> she is always one created in God's image,
> one whom God desires to heal and make whole,

> one whom God longs to liberate from sin and disease,
> one whom God so loved that he sent the Son
> > that she may have life and have it abundantly.

We should not, therefore, measure human lives
in terms of utilitarian calculations
of benefit and burden, profit and loss;
rather, we should measure human life
in terms of God's love for us.

We should not judge human life
according to our own criteria of
> biological viability,
> physical or mental ability,
> personal or social utility,
> or moral virtue.

Rather, we are to judge human life
according to God's unbounded, unconditional love
from which no one, *no one* is excluded.

Each and every human life,
> whatever stage of development, condition of dependence, or state of decline,
> whatever physical and mental strength or weakness,
> whatever usefulness to oneself or to others,
> whatever deeds done good or bad,

each of us—
> indeed, the whole world—

is the object of God's passion,
deemed by God as worth no less than
God's love given through the Son's life.

Set Free to Live in Love

This truth of the gospel message
sets us free to love,
free to "choose life"—
> and so free to value others
> according to God's own love.

And in so doing the gospel saves us
from being tempted into making several false choices.

First, the Good News that
    "God so loved the *world*"—
    the whole cosmos—
and sent the Son
    "in order that the *world*"—
        the whole cosmos—
    "might be saved through him" (3:16–17)
saves us from making the false choice
    between respecting human life
        and caring for all creation,
    between satisfying basic human needs
        and preserving the ecosystem
        we share with all God's creatures.

Instead, God's boundless love sets us free
to value all creatures as recipients of God's love
and to seek the shalom of the whole earth and all that dwell upon it.

Second, the Good News that
    "God did *not* send the Son
    into the world *to condemn* the world,
    but in order that the world might be saved through him" (3:17)
saves us from making the false choice between
    loving either the innocent or the guilty,
    loving either the victim or the offender,
    loving either the neighbor or the enemy.

Instead, God's unconditional love sets us free
to love and value equally the lives of *all* others
regardless of their supposed moral status—
    not just the unborn children,
        but their mothers, too,
    and also the abortionist and the terrorist,
        even the executioner.

Third, the Good News that
    God's love sets us free—

> free from slavery to sin (8:31–36),
> free from fear of death (11:25–26)—
> and gives us peace (14:27; 16:33)
saves us from making the false choice
> between security or justice or liberty or equality for some
> > and the very lives of others.

God's holistic love saves us
> from seeking security for ourselves
> at the risk of sacrificing the lives of others.

God's holistic love saves us
> from justifying the taking of one life
> in the name of justice for another life.

God's holistic love saves us
> from believing the lie
> that liberty and equality for some in society
> can be gained at the price of leaving undefended
> the lives of the most vulnerable among us.

God's holistic love thus saves us from
trusting in the futile liberation
and hoping in the false peace
promised by war, capital punishment, and abortion.

In his meditation on John's Gospel,
Jean Vanier,
> founder of L'Arche and co-founder of Faith and Light,
> communities for people with disabilities,
expounds the manifold dimensions of God's holistic salvation:[7]

> To "*save*" someone means "*to pull that person out of danger*" so that he or she is not hurt and a life is not lost. It means "*to liberate*" from oppression or "*to open the doors of a prison*" and let the prisoners go free. It means "*to heal*" or "*to make whole.*" Jesus came to save us from all those fears that close us up in ourselves. He came to liberate us and open us up to love. He came to give us the very life of God so that it may flow in us and through us.

---

7. Vanier, *Drawn into the Mystery of Jesus*, 86 (original emphases).

God's holistic love seeks to save, secure, and set free
our entire lives in Jesus Christ.
And thus God's holistic love sets us free
to serve the lives, liberty, justice, and security
of all persons equally.

Finally, the Good News that
    God so loved the world
        that "the Word became flesh and blood
        and moved into the neighborhood" (1:14, *The Message*)
saves us from making the false choice
    between evangelism and mission,
    between proclaiming and living the gospel.

Instead God's incarnate love sets us free
    to speak and enact the Good News,
    to flesh out the Word of truth,
    to live the life that is the light of all people (1:4)
        right here in our own neighborhood.

There is no choice to be made
    between proclaiming God's love for the world
    and joining God's mission of life and peace in the world.
Indeed, violence in any form is simply bad evangelism.

Which gospel of salvation does the church proclaim
when Christians support shedding the blood of America's enemies?
    Not the good news that God sheds his love,
        indiscriminately and disproportionately,
        upon both the friends and enemies of God's justice
        (Matt 5:43–48),
    not the good news that God shed his blood
        by the death of his Son
        for the sake of sinners
        while we were still God's enemies (Rom 5:8–10).

To which Christ does the church testify
when Christians advocate punishing death for society's sinners?
    Not the Jesus who shamed the condemning elders
    and pardoned the sinner,

"Neither do I condemn you.
Go your way, and from now on do not sin again" (8:1–11).

Which kingdom does the church announce
when Christians consent that the very lives of our weakest members
are not worth defending against the claims of privacy and liberty?
    Not the kingdom of justice
    in which even the least one among us
    represents Christ and the rights of God (Matt 25:31–46).

When Christians promote violence
    —whether war, capital punishment, or abortion—
the church proclaims a pseudo-gospel,
the church testifies to an anti-Christ,
the church announces a counter-kingdom.

To say it again, violence is bad evangelism.

Love in Truth and Action

Brothers and sisters, "let us love, not in word or speech, but in truth and in action" (1 John 3:18). It is not enough for us to say *No* to violence, to refuse to enlist our freedom in the service of the forces of death. We must go further and say *Yes* to incarnating God's love in our corporate life and in our community participation. God's love for the world calls us to imagine and enact life-affirming alternatives to the cycles of violence and patterns of tragedy that hold this world captive to fear and death. I thus want to conclude by offering some words of encouragement, challenge, and vision for the church.

First, words of encouragement . . .
Since 9/11 the United States has been so captivated
by a death-dealing cycle of violence and vengeance,
that I wonder whether the war on terror
hasn't robbed this nation of the freedom to grieve
and diminished its capacity to mourn the loss of life.

When the national leadership immediately turns national shock and sadness
    into a call for a national crusade against all evildoers

despite the pleas of the families of the 9/11 victims
that "our grief is not a cry for war";
when the President assures the American public
that the war deaths of American soldiers
are noble sacrifices to the national cause
that must be honored by yet further sacrifices,
and yet secludes from the public eye
the flag-draped coffins of the fallen heroes;
when the Pentagon describes as collateral damage
the deaths inflicted by the US military
upon the women, children, and elderly of other nations
and deems them not worth even counting
how is it possible for the people of this nation
to truly mourn these losses of life?

When Christian Peacemaker Teams reports back to us
home invasions, kidnappings of women and children,
arbitrary and secret detentions,
horrific tortures, sniper kills, and missile strikes
committed by the US military against Iraqi civilians,
it is hard for us not to be outraged or cynical
at such callous abuse of human life.

The church, however, is called to a different response.
A world caught in a death spiral really needs,
not more outrage,
but the freedom to grieve.
A dying world really needs,
not more cynicism,
but the hope that makes true grieving possible.

At times I feel that we are living
the parable of the children in the marketplace:
The present generation, Jesus said, "is like children
sitting in the marketplaces and calling to one another,
'We played the flute for you, and you did not dance;
we wailed, and you did not mourn'" (Matt 11:16–17).
Valuing life according to God's love
entails that we mourn the losses:

The Way of Life

      if human lives are worth God's love,
      worth even the giving of God's own life,
      then precisely on account of God's love
      each loss of life is worth our grief,
      whether or not the world will heed our mourning.
The church's mission to proclaim and live
God's loving cause to redeem this dying world
thus begins here, in our corporate worship,
with the prayers and petitions of God's people.

We already enact the gospel of life
      when we name one of our neighbors
      who is nearly overcome by a suicidal spirit
      and pray God's healing in his life
      and God's strength for those who minister to him.

We already enact the gospel of life
      when we pause to mourn
      the tragic death by suicide
      of one of our community's youth
      and petition the comfort of the Holy Spirit
      for his family and friends.

We already enact the gospel of life
      when we take our praying
      out of the pews and onto the streets
      to mourn a family desolated by domestic violence
      and petition God's mercy upon them and their neighbors.

The church's mourning is the protest of hope—
      hope that God's power of love
      is ultimately stronger than the world's powers of death.
The church's grieving is the cry of freedom—
      the freedom to trust in God's promise of liberating salvation
      rather than in the world's myth of redemptive violence.

If we were, in fact, redeemed by violence,
then there would be no sense to grieving the losses—
      each death would be necessary for our salvation.
If death were, after all, stronger than love,

then there would be no point to mourning—
    we should resign ourselves to reality.

Hopeful mourning, therefore, is protest in both senses.
When the church grieves the loss of life:
    we protest the lie
        that we save ourselves by violence
        while bearing witness
        to the story of God's saving love;
    we demonstrate against
        the dominion of death
        while proclaiming to a dying world
        that death shall not have the last word.

Like Jeremiah in the public square
    lamenting for his people
    because of their injustice,
like Jesus at the tomb of Lazarus
    weeping for his friends
    when faced with the tears of Mary and Martha (11:33–36),
the church's capacity to mourn—
    rooted in the story of redemption,
    sustained by hope of resurrection—
is the first, and perhaps most important, gift of love
we can offer to a dying world.

Second, words of challenge . . .

    Recalling the tragic story with which I began, it is evident that the world is in dire need of alternative, life-giving ways to address the needs of women in crisis pregnancies and to deal with the consequences of criminal behavior. And the good news is that the Spirit enables the church to model such alternatives for the world as living demonstrations of God's love.

    Many women seek abortions, not because they don't want to keep their babies, but for of lack of financial and material resources, absence of emotional support, limited access to affordable medical care and quality child care, or fear of harm from an abusive partner. That is, many unborn children are not unwanted, just unexpected. The church should thus be active in financing and staffing crisis centers and hospitality houses for mothers who need care and support for their unexpected pregnancies.

The Way of Life

    Our country's legal system metes out punitive justice based on the principle of retribution—determine who's guilty and then pay back the offender a punishment that fits the crime. Such a system not only fails to address the causes of crime but also neglects to consider the needs of victims. The church should thus be active in promoting the practice of restorative justice—a potentially redemptive way of dealing with crime that requires offenders to take responsibility for their actions, seeks healing for victims, mediates the victim-offender relationship, and seeks to repair the harms caused by crime to both offender and community, but outside the adversarial process of a court trial.

Last, words of vision . . .
I believe that the church
is to be a holy people that "chooses life"
in the midst of this dying world
that God so dearly loves.

I see a body reaching out
with the hands and feet of Jesus
to offer healing and hope
to a world torn by violence and hatred.

I see a community opening itself
to welcome and incorporate
as members of our own body
> women and children suffering domestic violence
>> or caught in crisis situations;
> neighbors who have suffered violation of their dignity and security;
> offenders who have harmed our neighbors and community;
> veterans carrying the hurt and horror of war in their minds and bodies.

I invite you to envision the church
as a redeemed people of God
for whom compassionate, peaceable, life-giving,
Christ-imitating, Spirit-enabled choices
are, with prayer and patience and hope,
both imaginable and possible.

9

I Am the Resurrection and the Life—

A Disciple's Politics

*I am the resurrection and the life.
Those who believe in me, even though they die, will live,
and everyone who lives and believes in me will never die.
Do you believe this?*

—John 11:25–26

*What are we to do?
This man is performing signs.
If we let him go on like this,
everyone will believe in him,
and the Romans will come and destroy
both our holy place and our nation.*

—John 11:47–48

The Way of Life

I wrote the initial draft of this reflection during Lent 2003. I was meditating on the narrative of Jesus' last days in John's Gospel, and my attention was drawn to the polarity created by the two figures of Lazarus, whom Jesus raises from the dead, and Caiaphas the high priest, who hands Jesus over to death. Lazarus succumbs to death, from which he is freed by Jesus; Caiaphas conspires with death, by which he seeks to destroy Jesus. Lazarus is subject to death, Caiaphas is lord over death—or so it appears. In truth, it occurred to me, it is Caiaphas who is subject to the power of death; it is Caiaphas, even more than Lazarus, who needs resurrection. Death rules Caiaphas even as he seeks to rule by death. And the only way of salvation for Caiaphas is death and resurrection: he must die out from under the bondage to death and be reborn through Jesus, who is resurrection and life. It then occurred to me that it is Caiaphas, rather than Lazarus, who is most relevant for the disciples of Jesus in contemporary America during the present epoch of ongoing war. War is itself a conspiracy with death in search of salvation, a conspiracy with which we in whose name war is waged are complicit. The gospel of Jesus—the good news of resurrection and life—thus calls us to die out from under the politics of death and practice the politics of resurrection.[1]

~

The Politics of Jesus

The good news of abundant life for God's people, made possible and accessible through the life, death, and resurrection of Jesus, is more than a merely spiritual message of little concern to the powers that be. In order to see the political significance of the gospel, we must observe this biblical fact: the canonical gospels uniformly attest that Jesus' death was arranged by human actors to serve human agendas. All four Gospels agree that Jesus was condemned by the state under a political charge ("King of the Jews"—Mark 15:18; Matt 27:37; Luke 23:2–3, 37; John 19:19) as the result of a conspiracy of the Jewish nation-temple leadership with the Roman provincial authority (Mark 14:53—15:39; Matt 26:57—27:54; Luke

---

1. My imagination in this reflection is shaped by Yoder, *Original Revolution* and Wink, *Engaging the Powers*. My exposition of the text here has been informed by: Horsley, *Jesus and Empire*; Cassidy, *John's Gospel in New Perspective*; Rensberger, *Johannine Faith and Liberating Community*; and Saldarini, *Pharisees, Scribes and Sadducees*.

I Am the Resurrection and the Life—A Disciple's Politics

22:54—23:49; John 18:12—19:30). All four Gospels agree further that Jesus was executed in a manner—crucifixion—reserved for insurrectionists, for those who threatened the security and stability of the regime, those who upset the *Pax Romana*.

Why, though, would the long arm of Roman power bother to kill a pacifistic rabbi in a backwater province of the eternal empire? Neither the medieval mind nor the modern mind is capable of an adequate answer to this question. To the medieval mind—which was shaped by the assumption of religious establishment and church-empire alliance, in which the imperial ruler is the appointed instrument of divine providence—this is incomprehensible: How could the ordained agent of divine providence have killed God's Son? Surely God had must have had higher, nobler purposes to have allowed such an egregious mistake, an apparent miscarriage of justice. Surely Pilate, the legal representative of Caesar's will, was only doing God's will by executing Jesus. The medieval mind thus constructed a supra-historical account of Jesus' death by divine arrangement—Jesus' death satisfies God's justice—to save the appearances.

The modern mind—which is shaped by the assumption of religious toleration and church-state separation, in which religion is privatized within the individual heart and the government is responsible for protecting individual rights—is equally incapable of comprehending it: Why kill someone for harmless, non-political speech? Why kill someone for merely personal beliefs? After all, Jesus didn't even have a party—he rejected alike the Herodians, Sadducees, Pharisees, and Zealots. Didn't that make him *a*political? In this light, Jesus' death appears as an irrational violation of civil rights by an illiberal regime.

The medieval mind, which understands Jesus primarily as the Cosmic Christ, misses the political aspect of Jesus—Jesus contra empire. The modern mind, which relegates all things religious to the private sphere of personal piety, misses the religious aspect of empire—empire contra God. Both the medieval and the modern interpretations miss the full significance of Jesus' death. And they do so primarily because both implicitly assume the same (false) dichotomy—that the church is politically either in control or irrelevant, either that the empire is the manifestation of God's reign on earth, or that the kingdom of this world and the kingdom of God are completely separate domains. How (asks the medieval mind) could Jesus the Cosmic Christ be any threat to an imperial order ordained by God and blessed by the church? How (asks the modern mind) could Jesus the

The Way of Life

obscure country rabbi be of any concern to the central authorities? Both the medieval and modern minds are thus unable to answer the crucial question that the cross asks: What had the powers that be to *fear* from Jesus?

As revealed dramatically by the fourth Gospel, the clash of the politics of Jesus with the religion of empire engenders a conflict leading to Jesus' death at the hands of the sitting Roman governor and the collaborating Jewish regime. For the human actors that conspired in Jesus' death, this judicial murder was no accident, neither a failure to discern God's purposes nor a failure to be enlightened by natural reason. Instead, the execution of Jesus by crucifixion, as well as that of the two bandits with him, was a routine terror tactic of the power politics of empire in the face of partisan resistance. Mass crucifixions followed the Palestinian revolts against Roman rule around the time of Jesus' birth in 4 BC and were increasingly used by the Roman governors of Judea leading up to the major Jewish revolt at Jerusalem in 66 AD. So, then, what had the occupying Roman authority or the collaborating Jewish nation-temple establishment to fear from Jesus? The fourth Gospel offers this answer: They were threatened by resurrection.

The chief threat to the powers that be—the rulers and authorities that lord it over the people, the systems of domination that oppress the weak and exploit the vulnerable in the name of peace and security—is *not* armed rebellion. Armed rebellion simply follows the same violent logic as the domination system, a logic that is sustained by fear and that generates retaliatory cycles of force and counterforce favoring the stronger side in the end. The powers that be employ violence—physical, psychological, and systemic—in order to instill and maintain a sense of fear among the people, a fearfulness intended to inhibit any inclination to revolt. Those who choose revolt resort to terrorizing violence to instill fear in the hearts of the privileged and powerful, a fearfulness intended to lead them to negotiate their survival or even bring them to their knees. Violence, then, is not a fundamental threat to the system of domination, but rather only reinforces it—the violent terror tactics of the rebel simply rationalizes the *escalation* of the physical, psychological, and systemic violence of the powers that be. Not fear-inducing violence, but *freedom from fear* is the chief force that threatens to subvert domination.

Case studies of contemporary nonviolent social movements show consistently that, even in situations of dictatorial rule and military repression, once a subjugated people no longer fear their oppressor, they have the power to withdraw consent from the system that dominates them. Active,

I Am the Resurrection and the Life—A Disciple's Politics

organized, and disciplined withdrawal of popular consent (by protest marches, civil disobedience, strikes, boycotts, etc.) can precipitate the fall of the system. This freedom from fear expressed through nonviolent movements has been described by political analysts as "a force more powerful" than the forces of violent domination.[2] Hence, the typical response of the powers that be to nonviolent resistance is to increase violent repression in an attempt to contain the conflict within the logic of domination, which ultimately favors the powers that be because they possess the greater firepower. This would explain why the tanks rolled into Prague's St. Wenceslas Square in 1968 in response to the peaceful movement for "socialism with a human face" and into Beijing's Tiananmen Square in 1989 in response to peaceful pro-democracy gatherings. It may also explain why an army bulldozer rolled over an unarmed international peace worker in (then) Israeli-occupied Gaza in 2003. Consider this observation of the Israeli-Palestinian conflict:

> More than a dozen international activists [working with Palestinians in the Israeli-occupied territories] have been deported [by Israel]. Many more have been arrested, and quite a few have been beaten . . . It raises the question of why one of the world's most powerful militaries would be frightened of unarmed civilians.
>
> While violent Palestinian resistance certainly brings real tragedy, it is obvious that it is not a real challenge to the status quo in this war. The Palestinians have neither the weapons nor the training to mount a sustained assault. The real battlefield of this war is the conscience of the Israeli people and the conscience of the world. And on that battlefield, resisting brute force with soul force is a winning strategy.[3]

In the politics of resistance to domination, overcoming fear is a more potent force, a greater threat to the system, than attempting to overcome domination with violence.

In the fourth Gospel, this chief threat to domination comes by way of resurrection; for resurrection liberates the believer from slavery to the fear of death. Fear of death is the ultimate dominating force wielded by the powers that be; thus, resurrection radically subverts the forces of domination. Resurrection is thus the ultimate threat to the domination system because it escapes the logic of fear and breaks the cycle of retaliation. Reflecting on

---

2. Ackerman and Duvall, *Force More Powerful*.
3. Nassar, "Palestinians who are working toward peace."

The Way of Life

his time serving with Christian Peacemaker Teams in the Israeli-occupied West Bank city of Hebron, the late Art Gish wrote: "The people who are in power are in power because they are not afraid to kill. The only human force that can overcome that oppressive system is people who are not afraid to die."[4] Resurrection hope creates a people who are not afraid to die—and, so, not afraid to resist. Resurrection, therefore, is a sign of liberation from the domination system, from slavery to the fear of death by which the powers that be rule the day. Resurrection signifies a potentiality that cannot be controlled, a hope that cannot be co-opted—an opponent that cannot be defeated. Resurrection signifies (potential) *insurrection*!

The Cult of Caesar

In liberating the people of God from slavery to the fear of death, resurrection precipitates a conflict with Roman authority. And it does so precisely because it challenges directly the religious claims of imperial power and the popular cults of civil religion. By the end of the first century, the cult of the emperor in Rome and the provinces ascribed three titles of acclaim to the Caesars: "savior" (*soter*), beginning with Julius Caesar; "lord" (*kyrios*), a title denoting supremacy, used extensively beginning with Nero; and "lord and god," specific to Domitian, during whose reign the fourth Gospel was likely written. The peoples of territories subjugated by Rome were forced to confess their loyalty to the emperor as "lord" and to worship the imperial military standard.

Counter to these religious claims of imperial power, the fourth Gospel offers an alternative narrative of salvation and lordship. All three titles that the civil religion ascribed to Caesar are ascribed confessionally to Jesus by speakers in the fourth Gospel: Jesus is "Savior (*soter*) of the world" (John 4:42), "Lord (*kyrios*)" (11:27), and "My Lord (*kyrios*) and my God (*theos*)" (20:28).[5] By the time the fourth Gospel was written, when the Christian community was experiencing persecution under Domitian, these imperial/messianic titles thus represented contested claims regarding revealed truth and ultimate reality—effectively, contested claims over sovereignty and deity. In his apocalyptic vision, John describes Rome as "a scarlet beast that

---

4. Gish, *Hebron Journal*, 284.

5. Subsequent citations of scripture in this chapter are from the Gospel of John unless indicated otherwise.

I Am the Resurrection and the Life—A Disciple's Politics

was full of blasphemous names" (Rev 17:3), referring to the exalted titles ascribed to the Roman emperors.

For the early church, the price of confessing loyalty to the emperor was committing blasphemy against the name of Jesus Christ and, hence, compromising faithfulness toward God. The reverse was also true: the price of confessing faith in (i.e., swearing loyalty to) Jesus Christ was committing blasphemy against the name of the deified emperor worshipped by popular cult and, hence, compromising loyalty to Rome. In reading the fourth Gospel, then, we should listen for undertones of politics whenever we find confessions of faith in Jesus and for overtones of religion whenever we find oaths of loyalty to Caesar. In the Roman ESmpire of the late first century, religious confession *is* political, and political oath *is* religious.

Resurrection proclaims a Lord other than Caesar, that Caesar is not ultimately in control, that Caesar is not God. Only one who is truly God, or sent by God, could work such a sign. But Caesar and the armies he sends to crush the will of the people bring only destruction and death, not resurrection and life. To believe in resurrection is to confess a God who transcends empire. To believe in resurrection is to confess a Lord higher than Caesar. To believe in resurrection is to proclaim that Caesar's sentence of death is not the last word, that Caesar's rule can be overruled. And to believe that is to deny precisely what Caesar claimed for himself—supremacy.

Resurrection thus sharpens the horns of the dilemma "Caesar or God" posed by the question of the imperial tax. Jesus answered that dilemma, "Give to the emperor the things that are the emperor's, and to God the things that are God's" (Mark 12:17). Perhaps it was possible to pay the emperor's tax and remain loyal to God. But it would not be possible to believe in resurrection and remain loyal to Caesar.

Jesus says to Martha, "I am the resurrection and the life. Those who believe in me, even though they die, will live, and everyone who lives and believes in me will never die" (11:25–26). What does he mean by this? We can see the implication of such a declaration by contrasting the words of Jesus with those Pilate says to Jesus during the trial. Pilate would say: "Do you not know that I have the power to release you, and power to crucify you?" (19:10). Pilate here speaks for Caesar, who says in effect: "I am ruler supreme. Anyone who denies me shall be put to death. I am lord of history and I have the last word on life and death." For all his boasting, however, Caesar can't do resurrection; while his governors and generals may answer his command to kill, the dead are not under Caesar's command. And Jesus' reply to Pilate, "You would have no power over me unless it had been given to you from above" (19:11), emphasizes that even Caesar's power over the living is not ultimate. By his word and deed—by claiming himself to be "the resurrection and the life" and by raising Lazarus—Jesus challenges Caesar's claim to supremacy: even the dead answer to Jesus' command.

Implicitly, then, we can hear Jesus saying to Martha: "I am Lord of life and history, even over death. Those who deny Caesar is lord, even though Caesar kills them, will live at my command." When Jesus then asks Martha, "Do you believe this?" he is asking for her undivided, utmost loyalty. She is thus faced with a choice, between incompatible claims of supremacy, irreconcilable loyalties, Caesar or God. Martha renders unto God what belongs to God: "Yes, Lord, I believe that you are the Messiah, the Son of God, the one coming into the world" (11:27). This confession of faith is, from the perspective of imperial authority and popular religion, both treasonous and impious. By it Martha professes loyalty to a king other than Caesar and declares that there is one and only one Son of God (and Caesar is not him!).

With her confession of faith, Martha has died out from under the domination system—Caesar has ceased to be lord. She has declared religious loyalty to Jesus—and thus political independence from Caesar. She is now a partisan more dangerous to the regime than any armed faction that lives and dies by the sword. For she walks in the hope of resurrection, which no weapon of death can overcome, and has thus been liberated from fear of death at Caesar's sword. The weaponry of the rebellious Zealots can be countered with the ever-bigger weaponry of the occupying Romans. But hope in resurrection is beyond the reach of Caesar's ability to crush resistance.

The Politics of Collaboration

The powers that be know this, all too well. The key figure in this story is, in a sense, neither Jesus nor Lazarus, neither Martha nor Mary. It is Caiaphas, the high priest. He himself is bound, a prisoner in chains, held hostage to the very power he holds, though he doesn't realize his bondage. He, perhaps more than even Lazarus, is in need of resurrection. Jesus tells Martha that faith gives life. Caiaphas is dead because he lacks faith. And he lacks faith because he fails to see that the future of Israel is present in Jesus himself, God's temple in the flesh, not in the stone temple built by Herod that he and the chief priests oversee.

I Am the Resurrection and the Life—A Disciple's Politics

Caiaphas's unbelief leads him to the wrong politics—Herodian-Sadducean politics, a politics of collaboration with Rome. Or, rather, the wrong politics leads Caiaphas to unbelief. Having been appointed by the Roman governor, Pilate, Caiaphas thinks that the politics of collaboration put him in control—that the security of the nation-temple establishment is in his hands as long as he, the chief priests, and the Sanhedrin render political loyalty to Caesar. "It is better for you," he proclaims confidently to the Sanhedrin, "to have one man die for the people than to have the whole nation destroyed" (11:50). Caiaphas is so ensnared by the cords of Rome's power, that he, the high priest of a holy people, willingly becomes complicit in Rome's sin, conspiring to have an innocent man executed to save the nation from Rome's wrath.

Caiaphas's conspiracy with death and hell crescendos when the Sanhedrin presents Jesus to Pilate for judgment. Pilate at first sees no threat to Rome and seeks to release Jesus, but the chief priests protest that Jesus is guilty of blasphemy: he must die "because he has claimed to be the Son of God" (19:7). "Now when Pilate heard this, he was more afraid than ever" (19:8). Why did Pilate become alarmed at the charge that Jesus was guilty of blasphemy under Jewish law? Perhaps because the popular cults of the civil religion claimed that Caesar is "a son of the gods." Was Jesus claiming equality with Caesar? Standing before Pilate, then, is not simply a pretender to David's throne (a matter in Pilate's view to be judged by the Sanhedrin—18:31; 19:6), but a potential challenger to the imperial throne. Perhaps to see if he really is "of the gods," Pilate thus questions Jesus' origins, "Where are you from?" (19:9). But when this question goes unanswered, Pilate tries to intimidate Jesus: "Do you refuse to speak to me? Do you not know that I have power to release you, and power to crucify you?" (19:10). Being the very one who is "the resurrection and the life," Jesus has no fear of Pilate's threat of torture and death and is thus free to remind Pilate that his power is not absolute: "You would have no power over me unless it had been given you from above" (19:11).

Perhaps sensing that he is accountable to an authority greater than even Caesar, perhaps sensing that he is in danger of trespassing against the gods, Pilate again seeks to release Jesus. But the chief priests again protest: "If you release this man, you are no friend of the emperor. Everyone who claims to be a king sets himself against the emperor" (19:12). Hearing his own loyalty to Caesar questioned and (implicitly) his political career threatened, Pilate without hesitation sits upon the judgment seat and presents

The Way of Life

Jesus to the chief priests for their decision, "Here is your King! . . . Shall I crucify your King?" (19:14–15). Having just questioned Pilate's political loyalty, the chief priests are trapped and can do none other than profess theirs: "We have no king but the emperor" (19:15). Rather than professing the imperial oath of loyalty, the chief priests should have recited the ancient enthronement liturgy celebrating Yahweh's universal kingship (Ps 99:1–3):

> The Lord is king; let the peoples tremble!
> He sits enthroned upon the cherubim; let the earth quake!
> The LORD is great in Zion; he is exalted over all the peoples.
> Let them praise your great and awesome name.
> Holy is he!

The chief priests' profession of the imperial oath of loyalty ("We have no king but Caesar") is thus tantamount to an anti-confession of faith that contrasts starkly with Martha's confession of faith in Jesus as Messiah and Lord. Whereas Martha renders unto God the loyalty that belongs to God, the chief priests render unto Caesar the loyalty that belongs to God. Whereas Martha's confession releases the fate of Lazarus into Jesus' power of salvation, the chief priests' anti-confession delivers the fate of Jesus into Pilate's power of execution. By convicting Jesus of challenging the emperor's supremacy, the chief priests convict themselves of blasphemy against God holiness. Now is made clear the consequences of the dilemma posed by Jesus' question to Martha, "I am the resurrection and the life. ... Do you believe this?" The chief priests recognize that faith in Jesus is incompatible with loyalty to Caesar. To save the status quo requires maintaining loyalty to Caesar, which in turn entails passing a death sentence upon Jesus. The politics of collaboration occasions the denial of God in word, which culminates in the killing of the Word of God.

Why, though, an elaborate conspiracy of Caiaphas and the Sanhedrin with unbelief and death? Because Lazarus is alive, walking around, on the loose, telling his story—and people are listening to him. If the confession of Martha is effectively treason, then the raising of Lazarus is tantamount to insurrection. Jesus raises Lazarus not in the private company of a few disciples and family members—no, this resurrection is public, with a "crowd" present. This is an open declaration that in Jesus resides a power that is even greater than that of the chief priest or the emperor. Before calling Lazarus forth from the dead, Jesus calls upon God in heaven: "Father, I thank you for having heard me. I know that you always hear me, but I have said this for the sake of the crowd standing here, so that they may believe that you

I Am the Resurrection and the Life—A Disciple's Politics

sent me" (11:42). Jesus thus demonstrates publicly that he has access to power that Caesar does not have, power to liberate rather than dominate the people: Caesar can put you to death, but Jesus can raise you to life.

In the synoptic Gospels, Jesus is tempted by Satan in the desert to seize the power of Caesar (Matt 4:1–11; Luke 4:1–13). In the fourth Gospel, Jesus is nearly forced by the people to seize royal power following the feeding of the five thousand (6:15). Then, Jesus resolutely resisted the lure of controlling power by which Caesar in fact ruled: with the masses enthralled by his ability to turn stones into bread or to feed thousands with only a few loaves and fishes, and with all earth's kingdoms under his authority, Jesus, like Caesar, could have fed or starved the people as he wished to keep them submissive and compliant. Now, Jesus manifests the true power by which God rules: not by enslaving the people to the fear of death, but by liberating the people from the fear of death, so that those who have faith in God's promise of resurrection might live to sing God's praise. Thus it was that Lazarus's illness led not to death, but to the glory of God—so that Jesus, the Son of God, not Caesar, "the ruler of this world," might be glorified (11:4, 27–32).

At Martha's confession, Caesar is dethroned. At Lazarus' raising, the empire falls. The confession of Martha and the raising of Lazarus send a radical message; and the crowd, even those informants who report back to the Sanhedrin and the Pharisees, get it. There is a power greater than Caesar—indeed, a power greater than death itself; and this power is alive among us in the person of Jesus. Many believe this message and act on it. As Passover nears, many of the people who had witnessed the raising of Lazarus go up to Jerusalem to look for Jesus in the temple, wondering if he would dare come to the city for the festival, apparently unafraid of the temple authorities despite the fact that the Sanhedrin had ordered Jesus' arrest (11:55–57). And later on, when the people learn that Jesus is back in Bethany for a dinner party, crowds come again to see him and Lazarus, too.

Indeed, on account of Lazarus's testimony, "many of the Jews were *deserting and believing* in Jesus" (12:11)—they were shifting their loyalties, switching sides, joining the Jesus movement. Upon Jesus' arrival at Jerusalem, he is met by a "great crowd" that had gathered for the Passover festival. They greet him with palm branches and shouts of "Hosanna! Blessed is the one who comes in the name of the Lord—the King of Israel" (12:13). This "great crowd" comprises both those that witnessed Jesus raise Lazarus from the dead and those that heard the testimony of the witnesses and

The Way of Life

came to see Jesus. And as Jesus rides into the city on a donkey, those in the crowd that followed him "continued to testify" (12:17–18). We can see here a growing opposition, a mass movement originating in Jesus' raising of Lazarus and growing by testimony of witnesses. Those that have witnessed the dead called to life by the command of Jesus, and thus believe that Jesus himself is "the resurrection and the life," won't fear the police dogs or the water cannon or the tear gas or the rubber bullets or the baton whack. This spells trouble for the nation-temple establishment, and the Pharisees know it: "You see, you can do nothing. Look, the world has gone after him" (12:19). The powers that be, which wield fear to keep the masses under control, cannot sit idly by while this movement spreads.

Unlike the Zealot rebellion, this is a peaceable movement; for the kingdom it seeks to establish, unlike Herod's or Caesar's, is "not of this world" (18:36). Thus, no weapons are to be wielded and no one is to fight violence with violence, not even to save the leader of the movement from arrest and execution (18:10–12, 36). Those who live by the sword die by the sword, and this movement aims to restore the life of the people. Even more radical than the Zealot rebellion, which caused many Roman and Jewish deaths as well as spread terror, this revolution brings the dead back to life! If Martha's confession and the raising of Lazarus signal the beginning of a "war" of nonviolent resistance, it is an upside-down war in which the forces of death lose decisively: not only is there no collateral damage, no innocent deaths in the name of national salvation, but the net number of dead actually *decreases*. Now that is a pro-life movement!

The Politics of Purity

Power and control are at stake for the Sadducees, who dominate the Sanhedrin. What is at stake, though, for the Pharisees? While not politically uninvolved, the Pharisees tend to keep their distance from the contaminating politics of collaboration—the Roman governor's compound is "unclean" (18:28). Instead, the Pharisees focus on moral righteousness, Torah observance, temple worship, and the purity of the temple itself (for which they are willing to risk suffering and death). Theologically, they are already convinced of the truth of resurrection; resurrection (at least in the abstract) is their (and Jesus') debate with the Sadducees (cf. Mark 12:18–27; Matt 22:23–33; Luke 20:27–40). Why, then, if they already believe in resurrection

I Am the Resurrection and the Life—A Disciple's Politics

and if they are more concerned with purity than power, is the raising of Lazarus a threat to their interests?

The resurrection to which religious orthodoxy attests is just the sort that Martha promptly confesses to Jesus concerning Lazarus: "I know that he will rise again in the resurrection *on the last day*" (11:24). Her confession refers to the promise of the prophets that there would be a "day" or "time" of final judgment upon the wicked at which God would vindicate the "righteous" and "wise" who have been slain for the sake of the covenant by restoring them to life (Isa 24–27; Dan 12:1–3). This, indeed, is the resurrection that Jesus also promises at first (6:44). That confession is fairly apolitical, for it poses no threat to the status quo: one can easily believe in a resurrection removed to the edge of history ("on the last day") and go on with things as they are in the mean time (so long as one benefits from, or at least has made "peace" with, the status quo). Resurrection "on the last day" demands no involvement with the movement of God's Word and Spirit in the actual course of history, no dirtying of the hands in the righteous struggle against real injustice.

Resurrection *here and now*, in the very person of Jesus ("*I am* the resurrection and the life"), however, is something else entirely. It disrupts the order of things as they are, revealing a new world order breaking into our midst. In this new order, the power ratio is inverted so that the power of God to restore the people—to make the dry bones dance! (Ezek 37)—is not only transferred beyond temple authority but transcends the legal limits of moral righteousness and ritual purity. To confess faith in Jesus and to follow him in the way of resurrection hope is to declare that Israel's life as God's nation has begun to be restored in Jesus himself—and thus that Israel's future is neither in the hands of Herod and Caiaphas nor to be secured through legal observance and temple ritual.

The Pharisees thus understand all too clearly the political implications of faith in Jesus and, hence, the implicit challenge to their position of separated purity. The politics of resurrection threatens the politics of purity as well as the politics of collaboration. Although the Pharisees maintain a critical suspicion of the Herodians and Sadducees, protecting their own position of purity depends nonetheless upon a stable, predictable collaboration with Rome carried out by others with weaker scruples. Were the Herodian-Sadducean nation-temple axis that has brokered the "peace" with Rome to be broken, the Pharisees' position of separation would no longer be tenable. Purity is parasitic upon collaboration; and those who make a "separate peace" with occupation are vulnerable without cover from those who profit from the imperial system.

The reality and message of resurrection thus upends the local *Pax Romana* in Palestine. This agreement was brokered with the Romans by the Herodians and Sadducees, administered by the chief priests and the Sanhedrin, and enjoyed by the Pharisees. It spared Jews the odious choice of whether to tolerate or defy the imperial cult and permitted the people's traditional worship *as long as* the latter was maintained within the ritualized limits of the temple cult and controlled by those whose status depended on Rome's favor. To allow Jesus and his temple-transcending, death-defying, nation-resurrecting movement to continue unchecked would be to tempt Caesar's wrath and put the nation-temple establishment in jeopardy. This is precisely the worry of the chief priests and Pharisees in the Sanhedrin: "If we let him go on like this, everyone will believe in him, and the Romans will come and destroy both our holy place and our nation" (11:48). Belief in Jesus, "the resurrection and the life," threatens the "peace" of the politics of both collaboration and purity.

The Politics of Death

What, then, is to be the response of the Herodian-Sadducean-Pharisaic alliance of convenience? They, of course, conspire to kill both Jesus and Lazarus (11:53; 12:10–11). Ironically, this would work *if* Caesar were lord over life and death and history, if Caesar's command to the living and his sentence of death were final and without appeal—that is, if there were no resurrection! Caiaphas's tactic to eliminate the opposition by violence is thus practical blasphemy, an act that implicitly affirms Caesar's claim to supremacy and denies God's authority in Jesus. But Caesar is not lord, and so Caiaphas's tactic is ultimately futile and self-defeating. When propagandist persuasion fails (12:19), the only response to resistance, even nonviolent resistance, that the powers of domination know is violent repression. But this response only betrays their weakness, for it simply creates opportunity for further demonstration that the forces of fear and death by which they dominate are not supreme.

The psalmist understood the weakness of the powers that be when he asked rhetorically (Ps 2:1–2):

> Why do the nations conspire,
> and the peoples plot in vain?

I Am the Resurrection and the Life—A Disciple's Politics

> The kings of the earth set themselves,
> and the rulers take counsel together,
> against the LORD and his anointed . . .

The psalmist could see that the conspiracy of the rulers and authorities of this world against the Messiah ("anointed") of God would prove ineffective. The fourth Gospel reveals to us why that is so. The plot of the rulers and authorities against the Lord of life is futile because the forces of fear and death, by which the rulers and authorities hold sway over the nations, are defeated. And the forces of fear and death are defeated because execution day in the kingdom of this world only sets the stage for resurrection day in the kingdom of God! The death inflicted by the rulers and authorities upon Jesus is only the occasion for a greater resurrection—and thus more witnesses, more testimony, more followers, a bigger movement.

This fulfills the meaning of Jesus' saying to his disciples at his entry into Jerusalem, after some Greeks came wanting to see Jesus: "Very truly, I tell you, unless a grain of wheat falls into the earth and dies, it remains a single grain; but if it dies, it bears much fruit" (12:24). The full-fledged purpose of Jesus' death by the powers that be, and the reversal of Jesus' death through resurrection by the greater power of God, is a harvest of "much fruit"—the raising up of a holy-living people of God from every nation: "And I, when I am lifted up from the earth, will draw all peoples to myself" (12:32). The draw of Gentile believers to Jesus as a result of the raising of Lazarus (12:20–21) is the "first fruit" of the great in-gathering of believers from all nations in a worldwide peace movement (the church) that testifies to Jesus, the crucified and risen Lord.

In a sense, too, all this is a fulfillment of the oracle of the prophet Isaiah spoken against Judah. The rulers of Jerusalem in Isaiah's day, like Caiaphas and the Sanhedrin in Jesus' day, had sought to secure the nation through lies and deceit. They had thus made "a covenant with death" (Isa 28:14–18):

> Therefore hear the word of the LORD,
> you scoffers who rule this people in Jerusalem.
> Because you have said,
> "We have made a covenant with death,
> and with Sheol we have an agreement . . .
> we have made lies our refuge,
> and in falsehood we have taken shelter";
> therefore thus says the LORD God,
> See, I am laying in Zion

The Way of Life

> a foundation stone, a tested stone,
> a precious cornerstone, a sure foundation:
> "One who trusts will not panic." . . .
> Then your covenant with death will be annulled,
> and your agreement with Sheol will not stand . . .

Jesus himself is revealed to be the "precious cornerstone" and "sure foundation" laid by God in Israel, rejected and destroyed by the leadership but chosen and restored by God. The "one who trusts" in Jesus for resurrection and life "will not panic" in the face of a death threat from the powers that be. The "covenant with death" made by Caiaphas and the Sanhedrin with the Roman authority through lies and deceit comes to evil fruition in the crucifixion of Jesus under Pilate's authority. But God's raising of Jesus annuls their "covenant with death"—and thereby lays the sure foundation for fear-overcoming faith and a new covenant of eternal life.

God's resurrection power in the life of Jesus convinces even the doubting holdout Thomas to commit his loyalty to God and join the movement, to stake his life on resurrection hope: "My Lord and my God" (20:28). Thomas's confession completes the self-stated aim of the fourth Gospel: "These [signs] are written so that you may believe that Jesus is the Messiah, the Son of God, and that through believing you might have life in his name" (20:31). Again, lest we overlook the political significance of this, we can hear Thomas as confessing Jesus as "My King." And we can hear John as saying, "I have written of resurrection that you might believe that Jesus—not Caesar—is the Son of God and that through believing in Jesus the resurrected one you may have life in his name even though Caesar puts you to death for confessing loyalty to God in the name of Jesus."

The Politics of Resurrection

How does this address us today? The resurrection politics of the Jesus movement, as John Howard Yoder observed, accepts none of the given options for engaging our political situation—neither calculated compromise (Caiaphas and the Saducees) nor puritanical separation (Pharisess), neither armed revolt (Zealots) nor quietistic retreat (Essenes). Instead, it is beyond both "establishment" and "sectarianism," beyond either being in control or being irrelevant. As Willard Swartley puts it, "The [fourth] Gospel's portrait

I Am the Resurrection and the Life—A Disciple's Politics

of Jesus is not that he is *apolitical*, but that he is *neopolitical*, transcending the disciples', the Jews', and Pilate's political categories."[6]

For us would-be disciples of the one who is "the resurrection and the life," resurrection politics first calls us to confess and repent of the ways in which we (like Caiaphas) have forged a "peace" with empire, made "a covenant with death and hell," or (like the Pharisees) have enjoyed a "separate peace," a purity parasitic upon collaboration. It calls us (like Martha and Thomas) to "die out from under the powers," as Walter Wink puts it, by renouncing allegiance to the arrogant claims of the powers that be and instead professing our exclusive loyalty to God in the name of Jesus. Such confession of sin and profession of faith frees us from the fear of death that enslaves us and enables us to live the new life of resurrection hope.[7]

Resurrection politics calls us to develop a biblical imagination that enables us to see the imperial system at work in our world and to develop the critical discernment that enables us to engage it both faithfully and fruitfully.[8] It calls us to hold fast to truth in the face of those who would claim unquestionable right and absolute authority for themselves and to speak truth to power to expose the lie of such claims. Resurrection politics calls us to zealously cultivate a consistent commitment to receiving life as the gift of God, a consistent ethic of life and peace that contrasts with and witnesses to a world on the path of destruction and death. We must therefore contend faithfully against every form of violence and every force of death that wars against the reign of God: rape, domestic abuse, abortion, infanticide, euthanasia, assisted suicide, capital punishment, torture, terrorism, war, poverty, racism, sexism, and ecological desolation. Resurrection politics calls us to nonviolent resistance to systemic forces of domination and structural forms of oppression that enslave the weak and exploit the vulnerable at whose expense the manipulators of the imperial system profit. It calls us to solidarity with and struggle for the marginal and outcast of the imperial system—to seek out those places and peoples abandoned by empire and build our homes and lives there, just as Jesus "became flesh and lived among us" (1:14).[9]

---

6. Swartley, *Covenant of Peace*, 286 (original emphases).
7. Amstutz, *Threatened with Resurrection*.
8. Brueggemann, *Prophetic Imagination*.
9. Here I have adapted the phrase of the New Monasticism, whose first mark is "Relocation to the abandoned places of empire." Cf. Claiborne, *Irresistible Revolution*.

The Way of Life

Most of all, resurrection politics—which trusts in the gift of peace and promise of life in Christ rather than the imperial "peace and security" propaganda—frees us *from* binding fear and frees us *to* sacrificial love and hopeful courage:

> Peace I leave with you; my peace I give to you. I do not give as the world gives. Do not let your hearts be troubled; and do not let them be afraid. . . . This is my commandment, that you love one another as I have loved you. No one has greater love than this, to lay down one's life for one's friends. . . . In the world you face persecution. But take courage; I have overcome the world! (14:27; 15:12–13; 16:33)

The Way of Peace

Come, O children, listen to me;
*I will teach you the fear of the L*ORD*.*
Which of you desires life . . . ?
Depart from evil, and do good;
seek peace, and pursue it.

—PSALM 34:11–12, 14

By the tender mercy of our God,
the dawn from on high will break upon us,
to give light to those who sit in darkness
and in the shadow of death,
to guide our feet into the way of peace.

—LUKE 1:78–79

As he came near and saw the city,
he wept over it, saying,
"If you, even you, had only recognized on this day
the things that make for peace!
But now they are hidden from your eyes."

—LUKE 19:41–42

10

Body, Soil, and Spirit—
A Disciple's Daily Labor

This poem reflects on an ordinary day of ordinary work on a farm in northern Indiana in the spring of 2003. The Iraq War had just begun with the "shock and awe" bombardment of Baghdad. In the months prior to the onset of the war, Christian Peacemaker Teams had sent a team to Iraq to stand in solidarity with Iraqi civilians, who would bear the brunt of the bombs. Those of us who supported CPT but remained on the home front organized marches, rallies, and vigils to protest the coming war.[1] After the bombing had begun, before the ground invasion, CPT decided to withdraw its team from Iraq to Jordan. During the overland journey across the desert of western Iraq, one of the vehicles in the convoy had an accident, injuring the passengers, some seriously. Amazingly, a car of Iraqi civilians from a nearby village stopped to help.[2]

Among those in the CPT Iraq team was Cliff Kindy, who was seriously injured in the accident. The Kindy family owns and operates a modest farm with vegetable gardens and chicken coops. While Cliff convalesced in hospital in Amman, Jordan, the usual preparations for spring planting at the Kindy farm fell behind schedule. Rich Meyer, a CPT reservist and Kindy family friend, organized a group of friends of CPT to spend a day helping out at

---

1. For representatives of my own efforts to resist the tide of war on behalf of the way of peace, see my essays "Pacifists have duty to be nation's conscience" and "How can the battle be won?"

2. The wonderful story of this incident is recounted by Barrett, *Gospel of Rutba*.

the Kindy farm. I had come to know the Kindys a couple years earlier on a road trip with Rich to participate in the annual protest at the School of the Americas. So, I was glad for the opportunity to lend a hand.

Practicing peace requires a faith community that not only is shaped by common conviction through the gospel of God but also is ready and willing to absorb the costs entailed by the commitment to follow Jesus in the way of the cross. This means that the discipleship community needs to cultivate habits of mutual aid and shared vulnerability that enable individual disciples to bear the risks of "the things that make for peace." Cliff, and his family, had chosen to bear the risk of practicing peace in a war zone; and now their fellow disciples were sharing the burden of that faithful choice by lending aid at the family's farm. The experience recounted here was the fruit of this habitual practice of the discipleship community.

This poem is slightly revised from the original text, which was published as "The Meeting of Body, Spirit, and Soil" in DreamSeeker Magazine (2005).

~

Your kingdom come.
Your will be done,
on earth as it is in heaven.
(Matt 6:10)

Bright sunlight unfiltered by any cloud
    spread its glory across a high, blue dome of spring sky
    as we trekked in Rich's well-traveled van
    across the flat, greening spaces of northern Indiana prairie.
Dressed and ready for work we were,
    having answered Rich's call a day before
    to share in the labor of the season,
    tending gardens and cleaning barns,
    alongside our sisters at the Kindy farm.
While sun and sky showered spring solace upon our heads,
    death and destruction rained from
    desert-dust-darkened skies over Iraq,
    defiling the soil with the blood of Ishmael's offspring,
    drenching the sand with the tears of Rachel's lament.

Body, Soil, and Spirit—A Disciple's Daily Labor

Our brother had left the family farm mid-winter
    journeying across dangerous frontiers and desert spaces
    answering the call from a voice crying in the wilderness
    to stand in solidarity with Iraqi brothers and sisters,
    to be a flesh-and-blood sign of the way of peace,
    to bear witness to the faith
        that God's reign
        is *the* reality
        on which we must reckon
        for our salvation.

> *Jesus came into Galilee*
> *proclaiming the gospel of God:*
> *"The time has arrived;*
> *the kingdom of God is upon you.*
> *Repent, and believe the gospel."*
> (Mark 1:14–15 REB)

The same call had fallen also upon my ear,
    but after prayerful wrestling my heart discerned that I should remain,
    to see whether, after all the centuries, perhaps the prophet
    might prove more acceptable at home than he did in Nazareth.
Now, as the next season of warring and planting was upon us,
    our brother lay convalescing in a hospital bed in Amman
    after suffering injuries in a motor accident—
        having been mercifully aided
        by the passing stranger who made himself neighbor
        along the bomb-wreckage-littered road to Jordan,
        and then graciously nursed
        by the grieving townsfolk and their doctor
        whose hospital sat devastated and children lay dead
            from bombing.
While bombs burst upon Baghdad,
    rendering buildings and bodies into rubble,
    we rendered heart, soul, mind and strength—
        shoveling manure, laying mulch, clearing debris—
    to build up the soil's life-sustaining power.
And as we bent our backs to the toil,
    our meager labor was amply compensated

The Way of Peace

       with the daily bread of earthy eucharist—
           the nourishing substance of spiritual conversation,
           the sweet odor of soil freshly turned from winter rest,
           tasty apple cake,
           soft warbling wafting on the gentle breeze through budding trees,
           cool, thirst-quenching water drawn up from the depths,
           more tasty apple cake,
           and the satisfying ache of a body tired from honest effort.

> *Do not keep striving*
> *for what you are to eat and what you are to drink,*
> *and do not keep worrying.*
> *For it is the nations of the world*
> *that strive after all these things,*
> *and your Father knows that you need them.*
> *Instead, strive for God's kingdom,*
> *and these things will be given to you as well.*
> *Do not be afraid, little flock,*
> *for it is your Father's good pleasure*
> *to give you the kingdom.*
> (Luke 12:29–32)

As I knelt down to pluck up and cast aside
       plant stubble remaining from last year's harvest—
       left in place to hold the soil in its proper place,
       to conserve with care the divine gifting—
the rain-softened ground hospitably received
       the pressing weight of my body-presence
       as if I were an expected guest
       invited to sojourn there awhile.
My grateful hands greeted the fertile soil—
       cool, dark, rich, sensuous delight,
       the primal stuff of the mortal being
       formed into flesh by craft of the divine hand
       and warmed into life by breath of the eternal word.

> *With what can we compare the kingdom of God,*
> *or what parable will we use for it?*
> *It is like a mustard seed,*
> *which, when sown upon the ground,*

> *is the smallest of all the seeds on earth;*
> *yet when it is sown it grows up*
> *and becomes the greatest of all the shrubs,*
> *and puts forth large branches,*
> *so that the birds of the air can make nests in its shade.*
> (Mark 4:30–32)

Then, there, amidst the grace-full meeting of body, soil, and spirit,
    parable seeds scattered in good ground,
    sprouting and growing we know not how,
    yielded grain ripe for harvest—
        peace with earth close to hand,
        peace with neighbors near and strangers far,
        peace with heaven and its Lord.
And looking up I saw
    the kingdom of God
        unveiled momentarily, elusively—
        like Yahweh passing by with a mountain murmur—
        here in this place where heaven and earth
        are joined with mortar of mundane toil and fellowship.

> *You cannot tell by observation*
> *when the kingdom of God comes.*
> *You cannot say,*
> *"Look, here it is!" or "There it is!"*
> *For suddenly*
> *the kingdom of God*
> *will be among you.*
> (Luke 17:20b–21 REB)

11

Body of Christ—
A Disciple's Communion

*The cup of blessing that we bless,
is it not a sharing in the blood of Christ?
The bread that we break,
is it not a sharing in the body of Christ?
Because there is one bread,
we who are many are one body,
for we all partake of the one bread.*

—1 Corinthians 10:16–17

Amidst the world's wars stands the church, the body of Christ, a visible sign of God's gift of peace to the nations. Yet the church herself has been a sign of contradiction concerning "the things that make for peace." Schism between East and West and divisions between Catholics and Protestants have spurred conflicts and sustained enmities. Because my own reclamation by Christ and return to the church was mediated by Catholic friends (see "The Way Home," above), I have a personal calling to ecumenical peacemaking—reconciling and healing a divided and wounded church for the sake of the gospel of Christ. Indeed, I have argued, ecumenical peacemaking is an evangelical imperative for the church: Jesus prayed that his disciples would be one in order that the world might see in their unity, in the love of Christians for one another, a sign of God's love for the world and thus come to believe that the Father has loved the world by sending the Son (John 17).[1]

The context for this story is Bridgefolk, a grassroots ecumenical movement of Mennonites and Catholics "proceeding through friendship," in which I have participated from its first annual gathering in 2002.[2] *Our institutional home is Saint John's Abbey, a Benedictine monastery in Collegeville, Minnesota. (This is only fitting, as Michael Sattler, who drafted the first Anabaptist confession of faith, the Schleitheim Confession of 1527, had been the prior of a Benedictine monastery, such that Schleitheim reflects in many aspects the Rule of Benedict.*[3]*) The heart of Bridgefolk is ecumenical exchange, in which Roman Catholics share the blessings of their sacramental practices with Mennonites and Mennonites share the fruits of their peacemaking practices with Catholics. The most obvious point where sacrament and peace meet is in the Eucharist, the sacred meal in which we receive and celebrate the grace of God through the life, death, and resurrection of Jesus Christ, who by the cross has united former enemies into one body and reconciled that body to God. Given the theological divergence and institutional separation of the Roman Catholic and Mennonite traditions over the centuries, however, the Eucharist itself became a stumbling block for us in Bridgefolk: Could we gather together at the Lord's table? This piece tells how the Holy Spirit, in a miraculous moment, graced us with a foretaste of the unity that is still our aim but is beyond our doing.*

This account is based primarily upon my own recollection of and reflection on the events related, but does include also some insights shared by others who participated in these events. The present version is revised from the original, which appeared in my article, "'Has Christ been divided? Was Paul crucified for you?'" published in Mennonite Life *(2007).*

---

1. See my book, *Atonement, Justice, and Peace*, 591–604.
2. Find Bridgefolk on the web at www.bridgefolk.net.
3. Concerning the Benedictine background of Sattler and Schleitheim, see Snyder, *Life and Thought*.

Body Discernment

"The Body of Christ." "Amen."
"The Body of Christ." "Amen."
"The Body of Christ." "Amen."

"The Body of Christ," Abbot John Klassen intoned repeatedly as he held up the sacramental host before each person who approached, hands held out in supplication to receive the sacred sign of grace incarnate, each one affirming, "Amen." This was indeed a day of marvelous signs.

Standing in the front row, just two steps from the altar, I listened and watched in awe as one after another of us stepped forward to receive communion, to partake of the one bread broken for us, to speak by our common ritual action that, yes, *we are* one body in Christ. The "we" gathered for this Eucharistic celebration was Bridgefolk, a grassroots ecumenical movement of sacramental-minded Mennonites and peace-minded Catholics, drawn together by the Spirit, each out of interest and respect for the tradition of the other. Our annual gatherings, always focused around a variation of the theme of spirituality and peacemaking, are occasions of mutual exchange of the gifts our respective traditions contribute to the body of the church catholic. We celebrate friendship in our one Lord, one faith, one baptism, and envision the future of a church unified and peaceable in the Spirit (Eph 4:3–6).

The events leading up to this shared Eucharist are too many to tell in detail. For five years we had struggled with the tragedy and sorrow of division, handed down from the past and poignantly present whenever we would gather for Eucharist with the monastic community in the Abbey church. How could we come together with integrity at the table of our Lord? We could not. Our Catholic hosts at Saint John's had made clear to us the rules for hospitality at the Lord's table in a Catholic context: while the priest could not openly invite Mennonites to share in communion, the priest would not discriminate among those presenting themselves for communion. Although stated with the best of intentions, this created an ambiguous situation for Mennonites: You're not invited to the table, but you won't be turned away if you come. It was effectively a "don't ask, don't tell" policy: We won't ask you if you're Catholic, if you don't tell us that you're Mennonite. So, should we Mennonites come to the table, or not? We could not honestly pretend to be Catholics and take communion before our brothers and sisters in Bridgefolk. Some Mennonite brothers and sisters, however, taking liberty with the ambiguity, did receive communion, causing offense to both Catholics and Mennonites within Bridgefolk. From a Catholic perspective, Mennonites receiving communion failed to show proper respect for the Catholic understanding that, by participating in the Eucharist, one signifies ecclesial communion with the Bishop of Rome, who is the sign and servant of the unity of the Church universal, as taught by the *Catechism of the Catholic Church* (no. 1369). From a Mennonite perspective, our decisions concerning the Lord's table were taken privately, each individual making up his or her own mind; there was no giving and receiving counsel among brothers and sisters, such that each of us was unaccountable to the other. Whether from a Catholic or Mennonite perspective, we were not "discerning the body" at the Lord's table (1 Cor 11:29) and the pain of division only multiplied.

But now, we were discovering recent developments regarding the rules of hospitality for fellowship at the Lord's table within the Catholic Church. In his encyclical *Ut Unum Sint* (1995), concerning the Catholic Church's commitment to ecumenism, John Paul II had rearticulated the criteria for non-Catholic Christians to receive Eucharist in terms that were more inclusive than the traditional requirement, taught by the *Catechism*, that non-Catholic Christians could be served communion only under conditions of "grave necessity" (no. 1401). Concerning specifically the situations that arise precisely in the context of ecumenical dialogue and worship, John Paul II stated that non-Catholic Christians could now receive the sacrament of Eucharist in special circumstances—*provided* that they greatly desire to participate in the Eucharist, freely request to do so, and manifest the faith that the Catholic Church professes in the sacrament. John Paul II repeated these criteria verbatim in his final encyclical, *Ecclesia de Eucharista* (2003).

We in Bridgefolk were just learning about this development at our summer 2006 gathering. Might this be a breakthrough for us, the breach in the wall of division for which we had so longingly looked? We took an entire day of our conference to discuss Eucharist, concerning the historic beliefs and practices of our respective traditions and concerning our experience of broken communion at Bridgefolk. We discerned prayerfully together what we might do in our future gatherings. Among the suggestions, might we: Focus on other "sacramental" rituals (e.g., agape meal and footwashing) instead of Eucharist? Develop an "ancient-future" ecumenical Eucharistic liturgy based on the second century writings of Justin Martyr? Develop a unique Bridgefolk ritual that would express our desire for full unity in Christ and yet respect our mutual traditions and their divergences? Begin gathering at the Lord's table for shared Eucharist under John Paul II's articulation of the criteria for ecumenical contexts?

If the latter, under what circumstances could we do so? Did the Bridgefolk context fit the intention of John Paul II's articulation of the criteria? Abbot John believed so. And what all is entailed by that third criterion, that the person requesting to receive communion "manifest the faith which the Catholic Church professes" in the Eucharist? Does that mean professing the medieval (Thomistic) doctrine of "transubstantiation," which the *Catechism* teaches is "the Catholic faith" and "has always been the conviction of the Church of God" (no. 1376)? Does it mean professing the medieval (Anselmian) "satisfaction" theory of atonement, upon which the traditional Roman Catholic understanding of Jesus' sacrificial death is based (cf. *Catechism*, nos. 615, 1362–1368)? Or does it mean professing only Christ really and mysteriously present in the Eucharist, the transformation of common bread and wine into "holy things" (per Justin Martyr), and that Jesus died "for our salvation" (per the Nicene Creed)? And, even if only this latter, would that mean also accepting the traditional Catholic understanding of "sacrament"—the bread and wine are not only a visible, concrete sign of God's grace made known to us in Jesus Christ, but also the instrument by means of which the Holy Spirit confers that grace to the Church—and, hence, that receiving Eucharist is both effective toward and necessary for salvation (cf. *Catechism*, nos. 1127–1129)? Our discernment left us with more questions than when we had begun. Yet, by the fact that we were actually discerning this question together it was clear that we had reached a breakthrough point, that a new Spirit was moving in our midst, though we did not know where it might lead us.

From Mundane to Mystery

Our immediate concern at the end of the afternoon was far more mundane and practical: Could we, as our schedule prescribed, attend mass at the local parish and still make it back to the Abbey in time for supper in the cafeteria? It looked unfeasible. In a fortuitous moment, a moment in which the Spirit moved unseen, Abbot John Klassen and Father William Skudlarek decided that, instead of us attending mass at the local parish as planned, they would celebrate Eucharist in a campus chapel for our Bridgefolk group. It seemed a reasonable solution to our practical dilemma—which meal, Eucharist or supper?

It is essential to realize that what followed had been entirely unplanned on our part, motivated entirely by practical concerns, without forethought for what might happen or what that might mean, for us or for the church. But, as we would soon realize, this decision brought about by circumstance would provide the opportunity for the Holy Spirit to do a mighty and wondrous thing in our midst, something we could not do for ourselves. Thus it was that we were about to receive an unexpected gift of God, an unforced moment of grace, of which we were all unworthy.

We quickly found ourselves gathering in the nearest available space, St. Francis Chapel, nestled between other buildings in a hollow of ground, secluded from casual view by a stone wall. The interior was intimate and plain, reminding some of traditional Mennonite meeting houses, reminding others that Francis is as much a spiritual ancestor of our movement as Benedict. We were too many for the number of chairs, so several of us took seats on the floor, on window sills, and on heating registers—a scene which might have been familiar in the home fellowships of the early church. I sat on the floor before the altar, just two steps away. The chapel lacking a vestry, we were amused at the sight of Abbot John, our presider, vesting in front of us—a rare sight for Catholics, even rarer for Mennonites! Amusing, yet appropriate—it felt as if we were all assisting him in putting on the vestments, in keeping with both the Mennonite and the Catholic (Vatican II) ecclesiology that the church comprises all the people of God (not just the clergy) and that all those "baptized into Christ" participate in a "priesthood of all believers."

We began the liturgy in the usual way—in the name of the Father, and of the Son, and of the Holy Spirit, under the sign of the cross—but we all could sense the unusual Spirit moving in our midst. What would happen? None of us knew at the beginning, of course. Many of us, including both Catholics and Mennonites, didn't even know as the liturgy began what choice we would make at the time for communion: receive, or not receive? Our discernment had not reached anything near a consensus on the question. For this reason, I had decided in my own mind and heart that I would not receive. While my heart held much hope for future possibilities, I was content to let the question remain open before us, to be resolved at a later time. I felt I could not, should not, choose to receive communion, not even in this context, without explicit consensus, without "discerning the body" (1 Cor 11:29).

Body of Christ—A Disciple's Communion

Following the introductory rites, we heard the scriptures read. The Gospel reading from Mark was the story of the woman with a flow of blood, who was healed through her faith when she touched the hem of Jesus' garment (Mark 5:21–43). Father William focused his homily on the Gospel text, pointing out to us how Mark's Greek, which piles up several participles in a row, heightens the scandal and shock of this woman's bold action: this having-bled-for-twelve-years, having-suffered-under-many-doctors, having-lost-all-her-money, having-not-gotten-any-better, having-heard-about-Jesus, having-approached-him-from-behind woman, *this* woman, *touched* him! How dare she do that! She was anything but "worthy" to touch him. And yet, by her touching him through her bold faith-in-action, she received healing through the power of Jesus' presence. From this story, Father William directed our attention to the Eucharistic celebration to come: in the Eucharist, he said, Jesus reaches out to touch us with his healing presence and invites us, worthy or not, to reach out and touch him and be healed. His homily left us in suspense, yearning for Jesus' presence.

In the prayers of the people that followed, among other petitions, we prayed for the unity of all Christ's followers and the peace of Christ's church. Thus was the air in the chapel filled with anticipation as Abbot John began the Eucharistic rite, "The Lord be with you." "And also with you," we replied from our hearts in unison. Yes, the Lord was truly present with us. After we had sung the *Sanctus* ("Holy, Holy, Holy, Lord God of power and might, Heaven and Earth are full of your glory, Hosanna in the Highest. Blessed is he who comes in the name of the Lord."), Abbot John continued the Eucharistic prayer. I watched in awe of the mystery of Christ's presence as Abbot John prayed over the bread and wine, recalling the story of the Last Supper and Jesus' gestures and words ("Take this, all of you, and eat it: this is my body. ... Take this, all of you, and drink from it: this is the cup of my blood. ... Do this in memory of me."). After we had recited the Memorial Acclamation ("Christ has died, Christ is risen, Christ will come again."), we all concluded the Eucharistic prayer with one great "Amen!"

Proceeding to the Communion Rite, we then prayed for the coming of God's kingdom with the Lord's Prayer and celebrated Christ's gift of peace to us through the sign of peace, which turned into a minor love feast all its own as we circulated among ourselves and exchanged manifold expressions of unity and peace in Christ. After we had sung the *Angus Dei* ("Lamb of God, who takes away the sin of the world, have mercy on us."), Abbot John gave the invitation to communion with great emphasis in voice and gesture, reciting the ritual words, holding high the consecrated bread and wine: "This is the Lamb of God Who takes away the sin of the world. Happy are those who are called to His supper." And we all responded, reflectively: "Lord, I am not worthy to receive you, but only say the word and I shall be healed."

In the midst of the holy moment, practical matters once again provided an opportunity for the Holy Spirit to break in and work wonders. As Abbot John stepped around and in front of the altar to serve communion, he suggested that in our small space it would work best to begin with the back row. Had I been one of the first in line to receive, I would have declined, and who knows how that might have altered the esprit d'corps. As it was, I would be nearly the last to receive, and I had a front row view of what would take place. What would the first persons in line do? Would Catholics decline? (Some had done this the previous summer, to express solidarity with Mennonite brothers and sisters.) Would Mennonites receive? No one really knew what would happen.

The first two persons in line to receive, perhaps appropriately, were a cradle-Mennonite who had become Catholic and a cradle-Catholic who had become Mennonite—both received communion. And through that the Spirit began to move in a marvelous way. One after another, both Catholics and Mennonites, proceeded up to the altar and received communion. As I watched in awe and beheld the mystery of Christ present in our midst, I felt the Spirit move in me and change my disposition, circumventing my all-too-human thinking, which still wanted a rational resolution to the question. At some point, as I looked on in fear and trembling, the Spirit made clear to me that, indeed, we were "discerning the body" of Christ—or, rather, the Spirit was "discerning the body" of Christ in us (1 Cor 11:27–29). And the Spirit's discerning led us to the Lord's table to share in the body and blood of Christ—so that we who had been made many by a history of division became, by the power of the Holy Spirit though the partaking of the one bread, one body in Christ (1 Cor 10:16–17).

As Abbot John concluded our Eucharistic celebration, "Let us bless the Lord," the air was filled with the Spirit as we responded heartily and joyfully, "Thanks be to God!"

Burning Hearts, Opened Eyes

In the days following, reflecting on this wondrous event, two biblical stories came to mind to help me interpret what happened. First is the Emmaus story (Luke 24:13-35). Like the two disciples returning from Jerusalem to Emmaus on that Sunday afternoon following the crucifixion of Jesus, puzzling over the meaning of the events of the week, especially the strange news from the women concerning the empty tomb, we also had spent the morning and afternoon of that Saturday puzzling over how to make sense of our situation, discerning what we should do next, wondering what John Paul II's articulation of the criteria for shared communion in ecumenical contexts meant for us and the church. And, like those disciples, on our own we were unable to satisfactorily figure out the matter before us. Then we began the liturgy—"The Lord be with you." "And also with you."—and miraculously, "Jesus himself came near and went with [us], but [our] eyes were kept from recognizing him" (Luke 24:15). Yet, slowly, the real presence of Jesus was revealed in our midst—through the powerful proclamation and preaching of the gospel, through the hearty singing of the people, through the Eucharistic prayer over the bread and wine, our eyes began to be opened. Suddenly, in the breaking of the bread on the altar, we saw Jesus, just as did the Emmaus disciples (Luke 24:30-31). After communion, as we joyfully conversed among ourselves, we could truly say to one another concerning the entire day, "Were not our hearts burning within us while he was talking to us on the road, while he was opening the scriptures to us" (Luke 24:32). And as each of us has "returned to Jerusalem" and gathered with our brothers and sisters in many places to tell about what happened that day, we could truly testify "how [Jesus] had been made known to [us] in the breaking of the bread" (Luke 24:35).

The other story is Peter in the house of Cornelius (Acts 10). Like Peter, we had been praying and were hungry (Acts 10:9-10)—praying for the guidance of the Spirit, hungry for full communion with one another in Christ (hungry for supper, too!). And we, too, had received visions that we could not fully understand. Some were seeing all of us, Catholic and Mennonite, being invited to eat together at one table—like Peter seeing all kinds of animals, clean and unclean, together on the sheet lowered from heaven (Acts 10:11-12). And upon hearing God call us to come and eat, some of us (including myself) balked like Peter, not wanting to do what had been "forbidden" (Acts 10:13-14). And others of us heard heaven's reply, "What God has made clean, you must not call profane" (Acts 10:15). So, while we pondered and puzzled over these visions, we sensed the leading of the Spirit that we should be prepared to respond to the invitation from God's messenger. The first messenger was Father William, who in his homily pointed us to the communion table where we could come and touch Jesus and be touched by Jesus in the mystery of the Eucharist. The second messenger was Abbot John, who invited us to the Lord's table, "Happy are those who are called to His supper." And so we found ourselves crossing the threshold into "forbidden" territory just as Peter found himself in the house of Cornelius. Many of us were saying in our hearts along with Peter: You know that we are not permitted to be here like this, but God has shown us otherwise, that God makes no distinction between us (cf. Acts 10:28, 34–35). Yet many of us were still hesitating in our hearts to receive communion—we needed to be freed by the Spirit. Just as the Spirit broke into Peter's sermon and fell upon all those who heard the gospel (Acts 10:44–46), so the Spirit fell on us who had heard the word—"Jesus comes near in the Eucharist to touch and heal us, worthy or not"—and set us free to come near and touch Jesus and be healed.

As I reflected later on what happened, I recalled the moment when, moved by the Spirit to the Lord's table to receive communion, recognizing the Spirit "discerning the body" in and among and for us, I let go of my need for a rationally-discerned consensus to guide our action as a body. And I thought of how Peter explained to the church in Jerusalem why he had baptized Gentiles in the name of Jesus (Acts 11:17): "If then God gave them the same gift that he gave us when we believed in the Lord Jesus Christ [i.e., the gift of the Spirit], who was I that I could hinder God?" Indeed, that is how I felt at that moment: If this be what the Spirit is doing in and through and for us this day, who am I to hinder God? And so, with those in Jerusalem who praised the Lord at Peter's report (Acts 11:18), I say again, Thanks be to God!

We are the body of Christ—reconciled to God through the cross of Christ and called to the ministry of reconciliation in the name of Christ. *Amen!*

We are the body of Christ—called to maintain the unity of the Spirit in the bond of peace. *Amen!*

We are the body of Christ—called to be one-with-another as a visible sign to a watching world that the Father has loved the world by sending the Son. *Amen!*

We are the body of Christ. *Amen!*

12

Jesus of Dresden—
A Disciple's Peace Offering

As a teenager, my consciousness—and conscience—had been pierced by reading the history of two events in the last months of World War II: the fire bombing of Dresden in Germany and the atomic bombings of Hiroshima and Nagasaki in Japan. I became convinced, years before being committed to the way of peace as a disciple of Jesus, that these events were horrific sins that morally demanded acts of atonement on the part of the United States. I knew, of course, that my country, which had prosecuted war crimes in both Germany and Japan after the war, would never apologize for its own atrocities in The Good War—such is victor's justice. If any atonement was to be made, it would take the initiative of individuals to make the journey to the land of former enemies and offer a sacrifice of peace. In May of 1997, at the conclusion of my time of study at the University of Cambridge in England, I had planned to take a tour by train of the European continent. That trip afforded me an opportunity to visit Dresden.

Returning to my earliest days of discerning Jesus' call, this poem reflects on my experience of seeing Jesus in Dresden—in bodies broken and risen, in churches burned and rebuilt, in brothers crucified and reconciled. My reflection is based primarily on memory, drawing out the impressions that the city made upon me then, and also on further elaboration of those initial impressions, drawing from my experience since. But, of course, memory is inexact, and the impressionistic details I recalled later do not necessarily match perfectly with empirical reality.

The Way of Peace

I wrote this poem in honor of the sixtieth anniversary of the destruction of Dresden on 13 February 1945. And I was privileged to proclaim this reflection on Palm Sunday 2005 to my brothers and sisters in Christ at the Lithuanian Free Christian Church congregation in Klaipeda, Lithuania.

~

> *Then he took a loaf of bread,*
> *and when he had given thanks,*
> *he broke it and gave it to them, saying,*
> *"This is my body, which is given for you.*
> *Do this in remembrance of me."*
> *And he did the same with the cup after supper, saying,*
> *"This cup that is poured out for you*
> *is the new covenant in my blood."*
> *(Luke 22:19)*

A heavy rain descended from a darkened sky
onto the streets of Dresden that warm, late spring afternoon,
sending up steam like smoke from the pavement
and people scattering for refuge from the rain.

I had come to make atonement.

Fifty-two years earlier, hellfire and brimstone had poured down
from the night sky onto the streets and people of the city,
    belched from the bellies of mechanical dragons
    piloted by British and American flyers—
        first high explosives to shatter structures into kindling,
        then incendiaries to set the rubble piles ablaze—
creating a fierce firestorm that literally sucked
the breath and life from the city,
    swollen with war refugees fleeing the Soviet advance.
Tens of thousands consumed, bodies and buildings—
    a burnt offering on the unholy altar of the god of war.

> *When you are offering your gift at the altar,*
> *if you remember that your brother or sister*
> *has something against you,*

Jesus of Dresden—A Disciple's Peace Offering

> *leave your gift there before the altar and go;*
> *first be reconciled to your brother or sister,*
> *and then come and offer your gift.*
> (Matt 5:23–24)

I had arrived in Dresden in the middle of the night.
The train had broken down along the way
and was late, six hours late.
Without a clue where to find the youth hostel,
I trekked from the train station across
several tram tracks and streets toward a lighted area.
A pedestrian plaza, I discovered,
all lit up but no one in sight. Eerie.
Just behind the plaza stood
aging cinder-block tenements, concrete signs of an era past.
My first crossing from West to East,
my first look behind the veil of repression
that Cold-War rhetoric named the Iron Curtain.
Fear shivered up my neck—
    like the security police could still appear at any moment
    and I would disappear without trace—
until I noticed the Burger King, and laughed out loud at myself.
Turning around I found a city map on a lighted board,
and soon was safely on my way to the youth hostel, just a few blocks away.

I began my city tour in the early morning sunshine,
heading across the plaza
where I had stood in fear just a few hours before,
now filled with kiosks and bustling with shoppers.
I visited first the Kreuzkirche—
    Holy Cross Church—
        its scorched interior left blackened for three generations,
        flaming shadows of memory etched into stone,
        testament to the city's endurance through trial by fire.
In the back chapel is placed a simple cross,
gift from the people of God at Coventry Cathedral in England:
Dresden's devastation was an act of revenge—
    eye for eye, tooth for tooth—total retaliation
for the destruction of Coventry and its medieval Gothic cathedral
by German bombing early in the war.

The Way of Peace

    This cross stands as a gesture of reconciliation,
    a sign of grace and peace
    from one fire-baptized faith community to another—
        to demonstrate hope in heavenly gifts of life and love
        greater than the hellish forces of death and destruction,
        powers that still master the fearful heart full of fury
        in this breathless night where rage fires of hostility,
        in this alienating age of darkness that is already receding
            before the dawn of mercy breaking upon us from on high,
            setting free prisoners from the valley of the shadow of death,
            guiding the feet of pilgrims along paths of peace.

> *But now in Christ Jesus*
> *you who once were far off have been brought near*
> *by the blood of Christ.*
> *For he is our peace;*
> *in his flesh he has made both groups into one*
> *and has broken down the dividing wall,*
> *that is, the hostility between us.*
> *He has abolished the law with its commandments and ordinances,*
> *that he might create in himself*
> *one new humanity in place of the two,*
> *thus making peace,*
> *and might reconcile both groups to God in one body*
> *through the cross,*
> *thus putting to death that hostility in himself.*
> *So he came and proclaimed peace*
> *to you who were far off and peace to those who were near.*
> (Eph 2:13–17)

    Later I walked past the Frauenkirche—
        the Church of our Lady, the Lutheran cathedral—
            a once impressive baroque edifice
            reduced by bombing and fire to a heap of charred rubble,
            left desolate for a half-century as a testimony to future generations,
            an anti-monument to capitalism and war,
            linked inextricably by socialist ideology.
    It was now just beginning to be rebuilt,
    raised from the rubble, stone by stone,
    with the aid of the British people—

Jesus of Dresden—A Disciple's Peace Offering

a testament of hope in the power of resurrection,
a monument to faith in the Resurrected One,
>who raises life anew from the ashes of war,
>who heals heart, body, and memory corrupted by hatred,
>who restores streets to live in and peoples to inhabit cities.

>*The spirit of the Lord God is upon me,*
>*because the* LORD *has anointed me;*
>*he has sent me to bring good news to the oppressed,*
>*to bind up the brokenhearted,*
>*to proclaim liberty to the captives,*
>*and release to the prisoners;*
>*to proclaim the year of the* LORD's *favor,*
>*and the day of vengeance of our God;*
>*to comfort all who mourn;*
>*to provide for those who mourn in Zion—*
>*to give them a garland instead of ashes,*
>*the oil of gladness instead of mourning,*
>*the mantle of praise instead of a faint spirit.*
>*They will be called oaks of righteousness,*
>*the planting of the* LORD, *to display his glory.*
>*They shall build up the ancient ruins,*
>*they shall raise up the former devastations;*
>*they shall repair the ruined cities,*
>*the devastations of many generations.*
>(Isa 61:1–4)

In the grey humidity of the warm afternoon,
the skies gathered forces to banish the sun
and the heavy air closed ranks around us.
And then the furious downpour.
I found myself taking cover along with others
in the entry way of the Hofkirche—
>the Catholic cathedral—
>>destroyed in the bombing but since rebuilt.

I had not planned to visit the cathedral,
but as the rainstorm intensified,
adding lightning and thunder to awe us,
I slipped inside to bide the time and have a look.

The Way of Peace

The usual baroque busyness—
    paintings, statues, altars, marble and gold everything.
Making my way around the sanctuary, I came upon a side chapel
and was drawn into a more intimate holy space.
It soon became apparent that it was dedicated
    to the sons of Dresden lost to war
    and to the victims of the city's destruction by fire.
After my eyes surveyed the memorial plaques on the walls,
the sculpture dominating the space took my attention captive:
    blocky, white stone, sparsely sculpted,
    arranged in several large pieces—
        a thoroughly modern work, I thought.
Though not aesthetically appealing to first sight,
I sat down on a bench to meditate on it.
I had time, so the muffled roar of the storm told me.
Other rain refugees came and went from the chapel
as I sat beholding this—
    what?—for several minutes.

What seemed like flames rising from hot coals
reached upward along the façade of one block, set in front of the others.
I wondered if the sculpture might symbolize
    the charred rubble of the city,
    washed white by the artist's imagination.

After further scrutiny, I noticed the sculpting on the largest of the stone
    pieces,
placed in the center of the work, set vertically.
At the top end of the block the coherent features
of a face became discernible—
    a woman's face, I thought.
Jagged protrusions radiated from around the mid-section of the block,
    as though shards of debris had pierced her breast
    like so many sharp swords—
        or, maybe she was exploding in anger,
        as if a delayed bomb, lodged in her heart, had just detonated.
It looked like her hands held
another stone block—
    a piece of the rubble, perhaps.

Jesus of Dresden—A Disciple's Peace Offering

And so I imagined this woman,
    kneeling amidst the ruins the morning after,
    lifting this stone as a prophetic sign
    of the shattered soul's burning lament
    wafting to heaven upon hands of smoke,
    rising like incense from the smoldering remains of the evening
        sacrifice.
But heaven, from which had rained hell the night before,
was now silent as these stones.

For several minutes more,
I pondered the sculpture overlaid by my mind's image,
lamenting with this woman,
    asking her—and God's—
    forgiveness for my complicity in this sin
    my nation had committed against her city that night.

    God, be merciful to me, a sinner!
    (Luke 18:13)

I thought my meditation and prayer had finished
when my attention shifted to the stone block to her side.
It, too, showed signs of sculpting,
    bearing marks resembling feet—strange.
And then I realized, it was another body:
    Oh God! I cried *sotto voce*,
        it's her child—
    she's holding her little child,
        whose lifeless body lies broken amidst the rubble.
    Her heart, bursting with angered grief, cries to heaven,
        perhaps even to accuse God
        for the catastrophe that has felled
        her child's life and her own hope.
    But though her war-ravaged heart is not yet hardened in defiance,
    her voice is muted, stilled within stone.
I sat to mourn with her in silence,
    waiting for God to answer her wordless prayer,
    for the tender ears of heaven
    to bend mercifully toward earth
    and attend to the interceding Spirit's visceral groaning.

The Way of Peace

> *Likewise the Spirit helps us in our weakness;*
> *for we do not know how to pray as we ought,*
> *but that very Spirit intercedes with sighs to deep for words.*
> *And God, who searches the heart,*
> *knows what is the mind of the Spirit,*
> *because the Spirit intercedes for the saints*
> *according to the will of God.*
> (Rom 8:26–27)

Suddenly, the image before me was reconfigured—
    a familiar form presented itself to my eye,
        and I recognized intuitively the traditional *pieta* motif:
            here before me was Mary,
            at the foot of the cross,
            embracing the pierced, broken, lifeless
            body of Jesus.
Yes, of course!—
    a mother holding her child.

As the broken pieces gathered themselves together
into sorrowful shape under my gaze,
    mystically transfigured into the body of Christ,
    tortured and twisted,
my own heart broke open
    for this woman, this child, this city.
And tears welled, overflowed,
tears for a mother mourning her son,
    bomb-crushed body, consumed in flames,
    flogging-shredded flesh, nailed upon a tree,
    life-breath exhausted, lifeblood drained—
        sacrificed blasphemously by human wrath,
        an idolatrous offering to the god of hostility.

The suffering of Dresden,
the passion of Christ—
    one.

Behold! Jesus of Dresden,
    Christ of the charred rubble,
    Christ of the crushed victims.

Jesus of Dresden—A Disciple's Peace Offering

Who would have believed what we just heard?
When was the Lord's power revealed through him?
He sprouted up like a twig before God,
like a root out of parched soil;
he had no stately form or majesty that might catch our attention,
no special appearance that we should want to follow him.
He was despised and rejected by people,
one who experienced pain and was acquainted with illness;
people hid their faces from him,
he was despised, and we considered him insignificant.
But he lifted up our illnesses, he carried our pain;
even though we thought he was being punished,
attacked by God, and afflicted for something he had done.
He was wounded because of our rebellious deeds;
crushed because of our sins;
he endured punishment that made us well;
because of his wounds we have been healed.
All of us had wandered off like sheep;
each of us had strayed off his own path,
but the LORD *caused the sin of all of us to attack him.*
(Isa 53:1–6, NET)

After some time praying there
in the intimate space of quiet agony,
I noticed sunlight filtering through the chapel windows.
I pulled my transfixed gaze away from the *pieta*
and my broken-hearted self from the chapel,
and left the cathedral for the wet, steamy streets.[4]

At sunset, the city cooled and refreshed
by the storm receding to the horizon,
I made my way back toward the youth hostel,
passing again by the Frauenkirche and the Kreuzkirche.
After crossing the plaza, again emptied of activity,
I paused to watch the evening shadows lengthen and deepen
against the aging cinder-block tenements—
    crumbling monuments to the ideals and failures of socialism,

---

4. The *pieta* in the Memorial Chapel of the Dresden Catholic Cathedral (Hofkirche), I have learned since, was sculpted by Friedrich Press in 1970–1973 using Meissener porcelain. One can readily find images of the sculpture through an online search.

The Way of Peace

        looking even more worn and tired in the twilight.
While I was taking a photo to mark the moment,
a young man approached and asked (in English)
        why I, only too obviously a tourist, would bother
            staring at and photographing such unappealing architecture
                (like, as I think of it now,
                    the men in dazzling clothes at the empty tomb
                    asking the faithful women why
                    they were seeking the living among the dead).
After we chatted briefly, and I related to him
the events of the night before and my experiences of the day,
        his bold question caught me off-guard:
            "Are you a Christian?"
        My certain reply to this stranger also caught me off-guard:
            "Ja, jahwohl!" ("Yes, yes indeed!")
He told me of the difficulty Christians endured under communism,
and of the new challenges to faithfulness—
        the advent of freedom and prosperity
            meant it was no longer so important to be a Christian.
He petitioned simply,
        "Please pray for us,"
and wrote down his name and address for me.
The sun having set, he asked where I was staying;
and as we were going in the same way, I joined him for a while,
he making use of my feeble German to teach me how to say this and that.
We parted into the night, exchanging the healing word
he had taught me to say while we walked together on the road:
        "Wir sind Brüder im Christus"—
        We are brothers in Christ.

I had come to make atonement that day,
but it was the grace of God that had granted me peace with my brother
through reconciliation in Jesus Christ,
who came near and went with us on the road.

    Now on that same day
    two of them were going to a village called Emmaus,
    about seven miles from Jerusalem,
    and talking with each other

about all these things that had happened.
While they were talking and discussing,
Jesus himself came near and went with them,
but their eyes were kept from recognizing him . . .

As they came near the village to which they were going,
he walked ahead as if he were going on.
But they urged him strongly, saying, "Stay with us,
because it is almost evening and the day is now nearly over."
So he went in to stay with them.
When he was at the table with them,
he took bread, blessed and broke it,
and gave it to them.
Then their eyes were opened,
and they recognized him;
and he vanished from their sight.
They said to each other,
"Were not our hearts burning within us
while he was talking to us on the road,
while he was opening the scriptures to us?"
That same hour they got up and returned to Jerusalem . . .

Then they told what had happened on the road,
and how he had been made known to them
in the breaking of the bread.
While they were talking about this,
Jesus himself stood among them
and said to them,
"Peace be with you."
(Luke 24:13–16, 28–33, 35–36)

Epilogue

Path to Peace—
A Disciple's Pilgrimage

*Too long have I had to live
among the enemies of peace.
I am on the side of peace,
but when I speak of it, they are for war.*

—Psalm 120:6–7 (BCP)

*Finally, brothers and sisters, farewell.
Put things in order, listen to my appeal,
agree with one another, live in peace;
and the God of love and peace will be with you.*

—2 Corinthians 13:11

The events of September 11, 2001 and following provoked me to reflect on my own path to the gospel of peace. I was reared in a Christian home and came to faith in a (fundamentalist) Baptist church, but was not taught to read the Bible from the perspective of peace nor encouraged to understand my personal

Epilogue

faith as a matter of intentional discipleship, following Jesus. And although I eventually came to grapple with the Just War tradition, the philosophy of war I imbibed at home and church was more a mix of nationalistic realism and American Zionism (i.e., the United States is the "new Israel" or God's "chosen nation"). The gospel of peace is thus something I had to set out to find. My searching was awakened by realism about both the evils of warfare and the possibilities for a nonviolent politics, and has been shaped by both idealism about the demands of justice and certitude about the transcendent value of human life. In following this journey, one will recognize an (unconscious) progression through multiple "varieties of religious pacifism" as outlined by John Howard Yoder, from Just War pacifism to Lordship of Christ.[1]

First drafted during 2001–2003, while the United States waged war in Afghanistan and geared up to invade Iraq, I offer this recounting of my personal pilgrimage with the prayer that it might encourage and guide others who also have been called to be pilgrims along the path of peace. Portions of this essay were prepared originally in 2002 for a presentation on "Christian Pacifism" to an International Peace Studies class taught by my friend Daniel Philpott at the University of Notre Dame. An edited excerpt from an early version of this essay was published as "Is Jesus Lord?" in Donald Kraybill and Linda Gehman Peachey, Where Was God on September 11?.[2]

Note: Readers will have noticed at various places in the preceding pages, and will observe in this concluding essay, an evident impact of the writings of John Howard Yoder on the development of my own thinking. Yoder was, no doubt, the most important Mennonite theologian of the twentieth century, the one whose writings have had the greatest influence beyond Anabaptist circles. I came to the Mennonite church in 1998, the year after Yoder died. I first read Yoder's magnum opus, The Politics of Jesus, *a year later. Only after I had read several volumes of Yoder's writings, and written many of the reflections appearing in this book, did I begin to learn, in bits and pieces, about Yoder's personal history of sexual offenses against women.*[3] *As this is a sketchbook from my discipleship journey, and as this essay recounts my pilgrimage to the gospel of peace, I must acknowledge the disparity between Yoder's writings*

---

1. Yoder, *Nevertheless*.

2. That short article has been republished online: http://www.thirdway.com/peace/?Page=1831%7CIs+Jesus+Lord%3F.

3. See the series of news articles on Yoder's sexual misconduct, which were written by Tom Price, published in *The Elkhart Truth*, and are archived online at http://peacetheology.net/john-h-yoder/john-howard-yoder%E2%80%99s-sexual-misconduct%E2%80%94part-five-2/.

Path to Peace—A Disciple's Pilgrimage

on peace and his own acts of violence, the former of which remain a valuable contribution to the church and the latter of which remain a real hurt to his victims.[4] While this is not the appropriate place to enter further into this matter, I do think that those who have an intellectual debt to Yoder's writings also share a moral responsibility to Yoder's victims to not only view his life in relation to his work but also assess his ideas in light of his deeds.[5]

•

Nascent Consciousness

My adolescence was marked by both cognizance of and confusion over terrorism against the United States: the seizing of the US embassy in Tehran in 1979; the bombing of the US embassy and Marine barracks in Lebanon in 1983; the hijackings of TWA 847 and the Achille Lauro in 1985; and the bombing of a Berlin disco frequented by US servicemen in 1986. Though I understood little of the history of conflict in the Middle East and the role of the United States in that part of the world, I was certain of the righteousness of the Israeli state and confident that the proper solution to terrorism was force. My mindset was one of striking back, as the United States did against Libya in 1986: we could not afford to appease the likes of Khadaffi the way we appeased Hitler, I remember telling my high school history teacher.

During the 1980s, the Troubles flared more intensely in Northern Ireland. This was soon followed by the Palestinian Intifada in the Israeli-occupied territories. Both struggles were played out vividly on television. I was shocked at the open, unapologetic violence aimed at civilians by Catholic nationalists in Northern Ireland. And I was quite unsympathetic to the rock-throwing Palestinian youths in the West Bank and Gaza. This was lawlessness, pure and simple: violence for political purposes is illegitimate and indefensible. The British and Israeli governments had every right to deal swiftly and severely with such terrorism: society must be defended,

---

4. See the blog post by Barbra Graber, online at http://www.ourstoriesuntold.com/2013/07/17/whats-to-be-done-about-john-howard-yoder/.

5. Regarding this responsibility, see the statement of Anabaptist Mennonite Biblical Seminary, online at http://www.ambs.edu/about/documents/AMBS-statement-on-JHY.pdf, and the reflection by AMBS president Sara Wenger Shenk, online at http://www.ambs.edu/publishing/2013/07/Revisiting-the-Legacy-of-John-Howard-Yoder.cfm.

Epilogue

I thought. Though largely ignorant of the history of the two conflicts, I was becoming sensitive to claims of justice. I was open, at least, to hearing about discrimination against Catholics in Northern Ireland; and I was quite opposed to the British government's suspension of civil rights for suspected IRA members. Still, I could not support their cause because it was pursued with violence. (I knew nothing at the time of the nonviolent Catholic political movement led by John Hume, who was later honored with the Nobel Peace Prize.)[6] I was not open, however, to hearing claims of Palestinians: Israel was Israel. At the same time, though, images of Israeli soldiers facing down, and sometimes shooting, boys throwing stones troubled me. The IRA killed innocent people with bombs. They deserved no mercy. These boys barely hurt anyone with their stones. Why shoot them? The Intifada dragged on: force was not working. I began to think of the situation in the Israeli-occupied territories by the analogy of pushing a thumbtack into a bulletin board: if the thumbtack is pointing outward, pushing harder will only draw more of your own blood and cause you more pain.

Then came Pan Am 103, destroyed by a bomb in 1988 over Lockerbie, Scotland, killing 270 people, including many Americans. When this crime was linked to Khadaffi, the United States wanted retaliation. Despite the horrific loss of life, and my personal anger, I was no longer motivated to see retaliatory violence as the answer: this called for legal prosecution, not vengeance. An "eye for an eye" would solve nothing. Indeed, this likely was already retaliation for our bombing of Libya in 1986 as retaliation for the bombing in Berlin—what would further retaliation prove? Prosecution would at least prove that law could not be undermined or circumvented through violence. As it turned out, thirteen years of persistent international law enforcement, backed by patient diplomacy and measured international coercion (e.g., targeted sanctions), succeeded without resort to violence in bringing two Libyan suspects to trial in The Hague, one of whom was convicted.

The year 1989 was a transformative year, not only for Eastern Europe but for me also; for in that year I saw the unimaginable happen before my TV-trained eyes. The Berlin Wall fell without a shot being fired. Communist regimes in Poland, East Germany, Czechoslovakia, and Hungary were dislodged without violence. We had been conditioned to believe that "atheistic communism" had to be fought with weapons of war, not of peace.

---

6. Hume, *Personal Views*.

Nonviolent politics thus became a practical reality in my imagination. I felt as if a deep but as-yet-unnamed hope was beginning to be fulfilled.[7]

Wars and Rumors of Wars

The 1990s opened with war. Iraq had invaded Kuwait. We learned the name of Hitler's latest reincarnation, Saddam Hussein. We must defend freedom and democracy, President Bush said. By then I was no longer naïve about such propaganda. I agreed that Iraq must be pushed out of Kuwait; international borders and national sovereignties must be respected and enforced. But let's not kid ourselves: Why was the United States defending Kuwait? Oil. It was the American economy that was at stake, not democracy—Kuwait is a monarchy, after all! Besides, the United States itself had unilaterally and unapologetically invaded Panama just one year earlier. The connection of this conflict to our own foreign policy was also becoming clear. We had shifted our Cold War support from Iran to Iraq after the Islamic Revolution in Iran (1979); we then armed Iraq in its war with Iran (1980–1988), and now Saddam was turning those arms against us. Moreover, we had looked the other way while he used chemical weapons against Kurds under the cover of war with Iran; and now he expected us to look the other way while he took over Kuwaiti oil fields.

President Bush said our fight was with Saddam, not with the Iraqi people, but our actions belied his words: we attacked bridges, electrical grids, food supplies, sewage treatment plants and water purification systems with immediate effect on civilians. We even deliberately bombed a known civil air raid shelter, killing hundreds of women and children, as well as buses full of fleeing refugees, including Kuwaitis whose freedom we were supposed to be defending. The destruction of civilian infrastructure and the killing of thousands of Iraqi civilians and retreating soldiers were unnecessary and immoral, as was the continuing destruction and death caused by sanctions and bombings. This force not only directly and indiscriminately killed non-combatants, but was also disproportionate to the narrowly specified United Nations-authorized aim of removing Iraqi troops from Kuwait (an aim that reasonably constituted just cause).[8]

The year 1992 saw the beginning of war in the Balkans, and with it came horrific ethnic violence in Bosnia and the ruthless siege of Sarajevo.

7. Swoboda, *Revolution of the Candles*.
8. Human Rights Watch, *Needless Deaths*.

Epilogue

I felt righteous indignation at the European Union, which was allowing carnage to go unchecked in its own backyard. And I was angry at the United States. We were willing to shed American blood, and even more Iraqi blood, to liberate Kuwait and protect oil supplies, but were unwilling to risk anything in the Balkans. Not only did the West not attempt to intervene in the early stages of the violence, but we imposed an arms embargo (through the UN) knowing that this would likely leave the Bosnian Muslims largely without capacity to defend themselves. I supported the 1995 NATO intervention—surgical air strikes targeted at select Bosnian Serb military positions and resources—that finally brought an end to the fighting and the fighting parties to the bargaining table, but mostly out of three years of pent-up frustration at UN/EU indifference. This was likely as close to a truly Just War as we have come in the modern period. Yet supporting violence, even at a limited scale, as part of the solution to conflict was deeply unsatisfying.

The 1990s were marked by the cowardly and immoral Clinton-era military policy: minimize risk of American military casualties at the calculable expense of killing innocent civilians of other countries, which gave rise to the pathetic cruise missile diplomacy that sent Tomahawks into Iraq, Afghanistan, and Sudan in retaliation for terrorism, resulting in dozens of civilian casualties. This policy characterized the US-led NATO approach to the humanitarian crisis in Yugoslavia in 1998–1999. Serbian forces were once again carrying out ethnic violence, this time against Kosovar Albanian Muslims. Some analysts argued that universal human rights trump nation-state sovereignty (an argument to which I was sympathetic) and, hence, that massive violation of human rights by a government constitutes cause justifying foreign intervention (I would have favored instruments of international criminal law and justice over blunt military force). Acknowledging moral failure by the UN in the case of Rwanda, and recalling EU reluctance to stop earlier brutality in the Balkans, NATO intervened militarily.

At its fiftieth anniversary, with the Cold War ended for nearly a decade, NATO had found new purpose as defender of human rights in Europe, so the propaganda proclaimed. In truth, NATO was concerned that a spreading Balkan ethnic-religious conflict would draw in Macedonia and, subsequently, Greece and Turkey, both NATO members, on opposite sides. This war was for the future of NATO, not human rights. In any case, after laying down non-negotiable demands that the whole world knew Milosevič would reject, NATO proceeded to bomb Yugoslavia. Madeline Albright, echoing Bush eight years earlier, said that NATO's fight was with Milosevič, not the Serbian people. But, as before, our actions belied her words. We bombed bridges, radio and television stations, water and sewage systems, and electrical grids, leaving the Danube River severely polluted. We bombed a railroad bridge as a passenger train was crossing it. We even bombed a bridge in broad daylight as people walked across it to go to market.

This war clearly violated Just War criteria: we deliberately pursued a strategy that not only directly targeted civilians (by targeting civilian infrastructure) but also put civilian populations at risk in order to protect military personnel. The NATO missions were flown above 15,000 feet so as to minimize casualties from ground fire, but at that altitude the smart bomb technology was no more accurate than conventional weaponry. The price of such self-interested carefulness was at least 500 innocent civilians killed, most of them Kosovars, the very people whose human rights NATO was supposed to be defending. Because at 15,000 feet pilots were often unable to even distinguish military targets from civilian objects (e.g., at least one caravan of Kosovar refugees was mistaken by NATO pilots for a Serbian troop convoy), a limitation in accuracy that was planned and accepted for the sake of avoiding military casualties and which had foreseeable and almost certain consequences for civilian casualties, the NATO policy of protecting its own before protecting the lives of civilians was tantamount to indiscriminate killing of non-combatants.[9]

Just War or just war?

I have come to believe that modern warfare, as judged by the criteria of the Just War tradition, is unjust.[10] This for me (initially, at least) is not so much a theoretical claim based upon demonstration from first principles, as it is an inductive conclusion from the weight of empirical evidence. Not even the so-called Good War was just. While a defensive war against German fascism and Japanese imperialism did satisfy the criterion of just cause, World War II was not waged with just means because the Allied strategy of obliteration bombing grossly violated proportionality and non-combatant immunity. The US campaign in 1945 of raining total destruction on some sixty mainland Japanese cities—beginning with the fire bombing of Tokyo

---

9. Human Rights Watch, *Civilian Deaths*.

10. For an overview and analysis of the traditional Just War criteria, see Yoder, *When War Is Unjust*.

and ending with the atomic bombings of Hiroshima and Nagasaki, costing more than one million civilian deaths—was the most heinous example of deliberate, indiscriminate killing of non-combatants via disproportionate force ever witnessed in the history of warfare. Nor even the US Civil War. While ending slavery may have been a just cause, the Civil War was surely not waged with just means. General Sherman's infamous march to the sea from Atlanta to Savannah and General Sheridan's scorched earth campaign in the Shenandoah Valley left wide swaths of near total destruction directed indiscriminately against civilians for the express purpose of demoralizing the Confederacy, thus violating the criterion of right intention in addition to non-combatant immunity.[11]

The accumulated evidence of the past 150 years (adding in the horrific slaughters and chemical warfare of World War I and the carpet-bombed jungles and napalmed villages of Vietnam would only strengthen the case) uniformly supports the conclusion that, in spite of (and perhaps because of) technological improvements, modern warfare generally fails two non-negotiable Just War criteria: proportionality (that the force used and damage done be proportional to the threat faced and the good gained) and non-combatant immunity (that innocent civilians may not be the object of attack). Indeed, in the wars of the last century, killing civilians and obliterating cities was no longer an unforeseeable and unfortunate accident of war but rather a chosen strategy.

Beyond practical considerations, Just War theory, I think, is untenable on fundamental grounds. Even though Just War forbids direct targeting and deliberate killing of civilians, the mere allowance for collateral damage—perhaps foreseeable, but unintentional killing of civilians, so long as such killing results from the use of discriminating force that is necessary for and proportionate to a legitimate objective—undermines the transcendent value of the individual human life. In biblical tradition (Torah), not only is the value of human life incommensurable with property (willful murder can never be compensated with monetary restitution, and property crimes never merit a death penalty), each person is unique and, as the image of God, possesses an immeasurable worth. The rabbis wrote in the Mishnah, "For this reason was one single human created: to teach you that anyone who destroys a single life is as though he destroyed the whole of humankind, and anyone who saves a single life is as though he saved the whole of

---

11. For a reappraisal of both the US Civil War and World War II from a peace perspective, see Juhnke and Hunter, *Missing Peace*.

humankind."[12] Moshe Greenberg, scholar of biblical law, comments: "The [human realm] does not consist of the sum of its parts. In the realm of human value each individual is worth the whole."[13]

Just War assumes either that one can subtract the evil of innocent lives lost from the good gained by violence to leave a positive result of good, or that one can at least compare the collateral damage done with the good gained to see if they are proportionate. If each innocent life lost is of immeasurable and incomparable value (and, indeed, is worth the whole of humankind), however, then such calculations and comparisons are not only meaningless but also devaluing of the individual human life. One innocent life destroyed is a loss that simply cannot be compensated by any good supposedly gained by violent means. Effectively, collateral damage is a utilitarian trade of innocent human lives for a justified end—and that is, in every instance, an immoral and unjust trade. Moreover, because judgments of the proportionality of collateral damage must in the end lump together lives lost and cities destroyed, the basic qualitative difference between the value of the human person and of material things that lies at the foundation of biblical law is effectively erased.

The profound respect for the transcendent value of the individual human life expressed in the Torah and Mishnah led the rabbis to raise the legal standard for the death penalty so high that it was practically impossible to impose a death sentence. At the very least, I propose that the standard for Just War be raised by eliminating that category of moral ambiguity—collateral damage—under which so much questionable shedding of innocent blood has been justified. No war can be just in which innocent lives are lost, for justice cannot compensate such a loss.

Recall the confrontation between Abraham and YHWH over Sodom and Gomorrah. YHWH wants to destroy the cities for their pervasive and grievous wickedness. Abraham, out of concern for Lot and his family, reminds YHWH that there might be some righteous people in those cities and boldly admonishes YHWH that it would be wrong for even YHWH to destroy the righteous along with the wicked: "Will you sweep away the righteous with the wicked? . . . Far be it from you to do such a thing—to kill the righteous with the wicked, treating the righteous and the wicked alike. Far be it from you! Shall not the Judge of all the earth do right?" (Gen 18:23–25). YHWH relents and agrees to spare the cities for the sake of only

12 Quoted in Greenberg, "Biblical Grounding."
13 Ibid., 50.

ten righteous persons. If collateral damage—here, the incidental death of a few righteous in the just punishment of many wicked—is forbidden to "the Judge of all the earth," if the rights of the innocent trump even the intentions of God, then what business of ours is it to justify even the unintentional killing of innocents in the name of combating evil?

Some may well agree that modern warfare cannot be just, or hold that war is never just even in principle, but still claim that, amid the sinfulness of a fallen world, war (and violence, more generally) is a (perhaps tragic) necessity in order to either save the world from evil ("redemptive violence") or fulfill the social responsibility of establishing justice ("realism").[14] I will briefly address these views in turn.

To those who would claim that without violent resistance to tyranny the world would at present be dominated by the successors of Hitler and Stalin, I reply: You assume both too much and too little. First, you concede too much to the power of violence, its potential for success and sustainability. In war, violence is (by definition) successful at most half the time (one side loses); and because even Just War often destroys the good that it aims to protect (collateral damage), it actually succeeds significantly less than half the time. Moreover, because it is necessarily founded upon lies and deception, and because everyone is suspected of disloyalty, a violent regime is not sustainable in the long term. As history shows, violent regimes (Hitler's and Stalin's included) tend to consume themselves because the principle upon which they are founded is neither creative nor life-giving.

Furthermore, it is precisely *because* ours is a fallen world that violence proves ultimately to be an either ineffective or unredemptive response to evil. Both history and scripture testify that violence has simply failed miserably as a practical solution to the problem of moral evil. The myth of redemptive violence, in particular, assumes that the earth can be purged of evil simply by identifying a certain group (the "wicked") and decisively eliminating it (via war, genocide, capital punishment, etc.). The line dividing "righteous" from "unrighteous" (if there is such), however, never cleanly separates the good-doers from the evildoers, for there is good and evil in every human heart. The biblical record confounds the success of redemptive violence. Even had the Israelites wiped out all the Canaanites in their conquest of the land, there was still the idolatrous lust in their own hearts

---

14. For the classic statement of the Christian "realist" perspective, see Niebuhr, "Why the Christian Church is not Pacifist." Elshtain, *Just War against Terror*, makes a case for the US war against terrorism from a Christian "realist" perspective.

that had already given way to human sacrifice before they ever encountered the false worship and foreign gods of unclean neighbors. Not only violence in the name of YHWH, but even YHWH's own violence fails to conquer sin. YHWH wipes out all the wicked of humanity by the flood, saving only the righteous Noah and his family, but soon enough humanity is back to its old ways of violence. And although Lot and family are spared destruction at Sodom and Gomorrah because they are righteous, Lot is soon committing drunken incest with his daughters. The only final solution to the problem of moral evil would be the total destruction of the human race, which is utterly unredemptive.

Second, so-called realism in particular concedes too little to the power of nonviolent politics as a means to resisting injustice and restoring justice. The history of the twentieth century—from India to Eastern Europe to South Africa, from Gandhi to Martin Luther King, Jr. to Nelson Mandela—testifies that patient, organized, and disciplined nonviolent resistance can (given time) dislodge repressive regimes without shedding blood.[15] In addition, successful models of restorative justice (e.g., Victim-Offender Reconciliation Programs in Canada, the United States, and New Zealand) and transitional justice (e.g., the South African Truth and Reconciliation Commission) show that society need not resort to retributive violence to do justice.[16]

The Lordship of Christ and the Kingdom of Peace

For me, ultimately, the morality of war is neither a practical calculation nor a theoretical argument, but a question of the call and claim of Christ: Is Jesus Lord? As a Christian disciple, following the teaching and example of Jesus, I am now committed to the way of peace. Simply put, the way of war, even a would-be Just War, is killing and destroying; and I find nothing in the life and teaching of Jesus that supports willful killing and destroying, much less training professionally to do such. There is much evidence to the contrary. Jesus said that it is peacemakers, not war makers, who are blessed and called children of God (Matt 5:9). He taught clearly that one is to love the other without distinction, both the foreigner (Luke 10:25ff.) and the enemy (Matt 5:38–48, Luke 6:27–36). When the disciples, having been spurned by a Samaritan village, asked, "Lord, do you want us to command

15. Ackerman and Duvall, *Force More Powerful*.
16. Philpott, *Just and Unjust Peace*.

Epilogue

fire to come down from heaven and consume them?" Jesus rebuked them: "You do not know what spirit you are of, for the Son of Man has not come to destroy the lives of human beings but to save them" (Luke 9:54–56). And, again, when the disciples asked, "Lord, should we strike with the sword?" to fend off the arresting soldiers, and Peter actually did so, Jesus said, "No more of this! Put your sword back into its place; for all who take the sword will perish by the sword" (Luke 22:49–51; Matt 26:51–52), and then healed the wound inflicted by Peter's sword. Jesus' love for enemies extended to forgiveness even of those who unjustly executed him (Luke 23:34).[17]

It is sometimes commented that, while Jesus counseled love of enemies and ordered Peter to renounce the sword, John the Baptist did not require the soldiers who came to him to quit the army but ordered them only not to abuse their authority (Luke 3:14). That is true. John, however, testified that the one coming after him—Jesus—would be the greater prophet (Matt 3:11; Mark 1:7–8; Luke 3:15–16; John 1:19–34). John pointed his own disciples to Jesus, some of whom then followed Jesus and went on to recruit more followers for Jesus, whom they confessed as the Messiah, not John (John 1:35–42). While some may wish to remain followers of John the forerunner, I have become a disciple of Jesus the fulfillment.

But Peter, who was a disciple of Jesus, kept his sword and wielded it against the enemies of Jesus in the Garden of Gethsemane. Why would Peter have a sword and actually use it to defend Jesus if following Jesus entails renouncing the sword? Doesn't that show that Jesus rebukes Peter, not because Peter has a sword, but rather because Peter misuses his sword (i.e., the same reason John rebuked the soldiers)? As shown in my earlier reflection,[18] Peter's possession of a sword correlates to his earlier confession of a false belief about the Messiah: Peter keeps a sword because he does not (yet) believe in a to-be-crucified Messiah (Mark 8:31–33). Peter's sword, as much as his words later that fateful night, therefore, is a denial of Jesus; Jesus' rebuke is thus directed at Peter's sword as much as at the false messianic belief that the sword is intended to defend. To put it succinctly: to possess a sword is to deny the cross, and to deny the cross is to deny the Messiah whose way is the cross; thus, to follow Jesus the Messiah is to take up one's cross, and to take up one's cross is to let go of the sword (Mark 8:34–35).

---

17. Regarding Jesus' entire ministry as a peacemaking campaign of "killing enmity" rather than killing enemies, see my book, *Atonement, Justice, and Peace*, 553–59.

18. See "I Do Not Know This Man," above.

Path to Peace—A Disciple's Pilgrimage

Peter evidently understood the lesson taught by Jesus at the garden, as he went on to exhort the church: "Do not repay evil for evil or abuse for abuse, but, on the contrary, repay with a blessing.... Those who desire life ... let them seek peace and pursue it" (1 Pet 3:9–11). Likewise, Paul instructed the church in his earliest letter: "Be at peace among yourselves ... See that none of you repays evil for evil, but always seek to do good to one another and to all" (1 Thess 5:13, 15). Paul thought this instruction so important that several years later he repeated it to the believers in Rome: "Do not repay anyone evil for evil ... live peaceably with all ... never avenge yourselves ... overcome evil with good" (Rom 12:17–21). And James, far from teaching that justice is the fruit of war, wrote, "a harvest of righteousness is sown in peace for those who make peace" (Jas 3:18). It is the uniform witness of the Evangelists and Apostles that the way to which Jesus calls us is a way of life, not death, of peace, not war, of loving others, not killing them or destroying their cities.

But Paul, while instructing the church to "live peaceably," also stated that the governing authority is the appointed executor of divine retribution upon human evildoers—and thus "bears the sword" in the service of God (Rom 13:1-7). Doesn't that imply that "living peaceably" and "bearing the sword" are compatible for the Christian? Nowhere in this text does Paul even imply, much less state, that any follower of Jesus should at any time "bear the sword" for any reason. Indeed, Paul says quite the opposite: God, in his wisdom and by his prerogative, has delegated the role of "bearing the sword" to pagan rulers; Christians, therefore, should never "take the sword" into their own hands to deal with enemies and evildoers—"Beloved, never avenge yourselves, but leave room for the wrath of God" (Rom 12:19a). The upshot of Paul's exhortation to the church is that vengeance is God's business—"Vengeance is mine, I will repay, says the Lord" (Rom 12:19b, citing Deut 32:35)—and not our business, period. In this respect, Paul speaks of Rome as Isaiah did of Assyria and Jeremiah did of Babylon: Rome is a "rod of wrath" appointed by God to serve the temporal purpose of restraining evil by punishing evildoers (cf. Isa 10; Jer 25). Christians are to "be subject" to Rome—and thus pay taxes, not foment revolt (Rom 13:2, 7)—but we are not to become Rome. What, then, is our business? Peace. As Jeremiah instructed the Jewish exiles in Babylon to "seek the *shalom* of the city" in which their enemies held them captive (Jer 29:4–7), so likewise Paul instructs the Christian believers in Rome: "If it is possible, so far as it depends on you, live peaceably with all" (Rom 12:18).

Epilogue

The Evangelists' and Apostles' peace witness was carried on consistently (in teaching, if not always in practice) by the church into the patristic period for at least three centuries. During that time, while there were some Christians serving in the Roman army, there are not only no extant sources endorsing military participation by Christians but numerous sources to the contrary. It is not until the legalization of Christianity by Constantine in 313 AD and the effective merging of church and state in 381 AD, when Theodosius declared Christianity the sole religion of the Roman Empire, that one finds Christian justifications of committing bloodshed in the service of the state (e.g., Ambrose and Augustine).[19]

On my journey to the gospel of peace I have encountered three chief strategies to justify bloodshed as permissible (and perhaps even dutiful) for the Christian, each of which relativizes the claims of Jesus as Lord by drawing some distinction foreign to the teachings of Jesus. One strategy is the medieval Catholic distinction between clergy and laity: clergy, who by their ministry imitate Christ's work of reconciliation on the cross, are to be willing to have their own blood shed rather than to shed blood and, hence, ought not participate in war; in commanding Peter to put away the sword, Jesus disarmed only clergy, not laity.[20] Jesus, however, makes no such distinction in his command, "Be perfect, therefore, as your heavenly Father is perfect" (Matt 5:48); indeed, he commanded Peter to sheath the sword because "*all* who take the sword will perish by the sword" (Matt 26:52). Moreover, according to Paul, *all* those who have been reconciled to God through Christ share in Christ's "ministry of reconciliation" as "ambassadors of Christ" to whom has been committed "the message of reconciliation" (2 Cor 5:18–20). The ethical distinction between clergy and laity was effectively erased by the Second Vatican Council of the Catholic Church, which proclaimed that *all* Christians, by virtue of our baptism (and confirmation), are called to conversion, discipleship, and a life of holiness in the world. The gospel of life and the way of peace, the Council declared, is the proper vocation of laity and clergy alike.

A second, more recent, strategy is dispensationalism (popular among Evangelicals), which holds that the gospel either simply fulfills the age of law (e.g., the Sermon on the Mount), so that the law of perfect love is relevant only to Jesus himself, or points to a future heavenly kingdom in which

---

19. For early church views on Christian participation in the military, see Hornus, *It Is Not Lawful for Me to Fight* and Bainton, *Christian Attitudes toward War and Peace*.

20. See Aquinas, *Summa Theologiae*, II-II, Q. 40, A. 2.

love will rule perfectly.[21] In either case, the gospel is not relevant to us in the age of grace. Jesus, however, instructed his disciples to seek God's reign first (Matt 6:33) and to pray for the reign of God on earth as in heaven (Matt 6:10)—here, now. And Paul, herald of the age of grace, declared himself to be "under Christ's law" (1 Cor 9:21) and instructed us to "fulfill the law of Christ" (Gal 6:2).

Third is the Augustinian-Lutheran two-office or two-vocation version of two-kingdom theology, a mainstay of Protestantism, which distinguishes between the Christian acting privately as a member of the church and acting publicly as a citizen of the state. God has instituted two equally legitimate kingdoms—one spiritual, which commands the heart and mind according to the gospel law of love, the other political, which commands the body according to the civic law of the sword—and we are to do service to God through obedience to both.[22] Thus, while on Sunday as a Christian believer I am to love my neighbor in the name of Jesus, on Monday as a citizen officer or soldier I am permitted (and sometimes even dutifully bound) to kill both my fellow citizen in the name of public order and the foreign enemy in the name of national defense (to the extent that natural law justice allows).

Again, there is no basis for such a distinction in the gospel: Jesus did not preach a public morality over and against a private morality, one morality for Sunday and another for the rest of the week. Moreover, this strategy engenders a dichotomy between the inner/spiritual person (a mind that thinks and a heart that feels) and the outer/political agent (a body that speaks and acts), one who loves in the heart while the other kills with the hands. This is an ethical and existential self-division that violates the basic integrity of the human person and that Jesus rejected: blessed is the one who is *both* pure in heart *and* a peacemaker (Matt 5:8–9; cf. Matt 5:21–26). Jesus did say that we are to "Give to the emperor the things that are the emperor's," but he promptly added that we are to "give to God the things that are God's" (Matt 22:21). Coins may belong to Caesar, but the rest belongs to God according to the old commandment: "love the Lord your God with all your heart, and with all your soul, and with all your mind, and with all your strength" (Mark 12:28–30). Not just my spirit, but also the capacities of my body—and thus all my actions—belong *wholly* to God.

---

21. See the introductory essay to the Gospels and the notes to Genesis 1 and Matthew 5 in C. I. Scofield's reference edition of the Authorized King James Version of the Bible.

22. See Augustine, *Reply to Faustus* and Luther, "Whether Soldiers, Too, Can Be Saved."

Epilogue

Similarly, while Paul and Peter affirmed that we should subordinate ourselves to governing authority (Rom 13:1–7; 1 Pet 2:13–18), they further explained that we are to do so for the sake of maintaining a peaceable witness among the nations. Upon sanctioning us to "give to each what is due," Paul clearly stated that we are under no other obligation "except to love," which "does no wrong to a neighbor" (Rom 13:8–10). And Peter explicitly linked subordination to authority with suffering for the sake of Christ, not killing for the sake of nation-state (1 Pet 2:19–21). Furthermore, nowhere did they say or imply that we are to obey the authority of the state without regard for the teachings of Jesus. Indeed, Paul instructed us: "Only, live your life in a manner worthy of the gospel of Christ" (Phil 1:27).

Finally, latent within this Protestant two-kingdom strategy is the absurdly tragic outcome that fellow Christians who happen to be citizens of different nation-states might both serve God by killing one another in obedience to their respective earthly rulers, both of whom claim to be on the side of justice. Such an outcome would utterly mock Jesus' prayer for the unity of his followers in love (John 17:20–23) and flagrantly breach the unity of the church as the body of Christ in which former enemies are reconciled to each other and to God by one Spirit through the peace of the cross (Eph 2:11–22).

To each of these strategies I reply as did Jesus to the Pharisees regarding the oral traditions that they added to the Torah and used to heap burdens upon the people: "You abandon the commandment of God and hold to human tradition. . . . thus making void the word of God through your tradition that you have handed on" (Mark 7:8, 13).

There is, in truth, only *one* kingdom having an absolute right to command obedience. This kingdom of universal reign has one Sovereign, Jesus Christ the risen Lord (Luke 2:11; Matt 28:18; Acts 2:36, 10:36; Phil 2:9–11; Rev 11:15). Baptized believers have common citizenship under this one sovereignty (Eph 2:19; Phil 3:20)—a citizenship that transcends nation-state citizenship, a sovereignty that trumps nation-state sovereignty. Just War theory states that the moral right to wage war is invested in legitimate authority. For the Christian disciple, Jesus is the one and only legitimate authority whose word is our command, whom we must obey—before, besides, and beyond any and all human authority (Acts 5:29). Subject without qualification to Jesus as Lord, the disciple may commit violence and bloodshed in obedience to the lords of this world for the sake of any cause *if and only if* he can do so in the name of Jesus. The consistent witness of Evangelists and Apostles, which calls the disciple to imitate Jesus, who was himself "obedient to the point of death" (Matt 10:38–39; 17:24–26; Eph 5:1–2; Phil 2:5–8; 1 Pet 2:19–23), makes plain that to kill in the name of Jesus would be simply blasphemous.[23]

What about . . .

. . . The Old Testament?

At this point, one may well want to ask, and appropriately so: What about the Old Testament? Doesn't it give precedent for participation in war by God's people as an expression of faithfulness to God's justice and righteousness? Doesn't this show not only that peace is not the necessary duty of Christians, but perhaps just the opposite, that war might be a duty? While I have no easy answer to this serious question, much less a comprehensive view of how to interpret the Old Testament in light of the gospel of peace revealed in Jesus, I offer some observations that challenge the use of wars in the Old Testament as moral precedents for Christian practice.

First, the gospel of peace revealed in Jesus has roots as deep as the Old Testament itself, finding manifold expression in the Torah, Prophets, Psalms, and Wisdom writings. Indeed, the Prophets, Jesus, and the Apostles are linked by a consistent thread following the theme of God's messenger (or evangelist) of "good news of peace," tracing a development that finds its fullness in Jesus and, by extension, in the Apostles and Prophets of the church. The gospel of peace thus represents a major strand of the faith tradition handed down within Israel for centuries prior to Jesus and finds its authentic place at the heart of God's covenant with his people. Peace is not only not peripheral to the New Testament, it is not peripheral to the Old Testament, either. That the gospel of peace finds a natural home within the Old Testament ought to guide how we, the church, read these scriptures and shape how we interpret their contemporary relevance for the church.[24]

---

23. For further argument that following in the way of Jesus entails renouncing the way of war, see my book, *Atonement, Justice, and Peace*, 531–41, 616–29. I have not attempted here to deal with every text or answer every question concerning the New Testament witness against violence. For a careful treatment of a wide range of texts and questions on this matter, see Sprinkle, *Fight*.

24. Yoder, *Shalom*, considers peace as a concept comprehending the entire biblical canon. Mauser, *Gospel of Peace* and Swartley, *Covenant of Peace* each consider peace as a unifying concept of the New Testament. See also my book, *Good News*, which elaborates

Epilogue

Second, if war is to be a moral cause, and if wars past are to serve as precedent for present moral judgment, then war must be waged within certain moral limits. Unlimited warfare is simply evil. The Torah itself spells out rules of warfare to govern the Israelites when summoned by God to fight (Deut 20). The context motivating such a Holy War code is evidently the military conquest of Canaan led by Joshua. This code for waging Holy War offers exemption from military service to certain groups, provides for peaceful negotiation with the enemy prior to fighting, limits the destruction of war to some extent, and gives some (though significantly limited) recognition to non-combatants (women and children) but not prisoners of war. Unlike Just War, which presumes a posture of defense against aggression, the Holy War rules presume an aggressive stance on the part of the Israelites (cf. vv. 10, 19). This aggressive stance, of course, befits the Holy War motif: if God has summoned us to fight (through the figure of the priest, v. 2), there is no further need to justify violence and, hence, the offensive may (indeed, must) be taken against the enemy even without provocation (the summons of God is cause enough for war); and if God has justified our violence, then no human moral limits apply (the only limit is God's will).[25]

Now, if one takes a careful look at the wars of conquest as depicted in Joshua 6–11, one will find that these rules simply were not followed in any systematic manner. Israelite Holy Wars in the name of God violated the Torah's own code of war in various respects. This throws a major interpretive stumbling block in the way of using the Israelite Holy War tradition as moral precedent for contemporary Christian practice: Is the fact that the biblical canon preserves the narrative of a whole series of Israelite *violation* of the code of warfare evidence only of the unfaithfulness of the people in conducting warfare—or is it evidence of the illegitimacy of God's people participating in warfare in God's name? Is this only a reinforcement of Holy War through counterexample—or is it a subtle subversion of the very idea of Holy War in the Old Testament?

In any case, third, Christian tradition has over the centuries soundly rejected Holy War as an acceptable paradigm for participation in war as a moral cause, developing in its place the Just War theory. Against the moral framework of Just War, the Israelite wars in the Old Testament look even

---

the connection between the message of peace in the Gospel of Luke and the message of salvation in the Prophets and Psalms.

25. For an excellent study of war in the Old Testament, see Niditch, *War in the Hebrew Bible*.

Path to Peace—A Disciple's Pilgrimage

worse. The vast majority of Israelite wars, including most of those depicted as Holy War sanctioned by God, egregiously violated the traditional Just War criteria. Most of the wars were clearly aggressive, did not give peaceful negotiations a chance, failed to grant immunity to non-combatants (women and children were slaughtered along with the male warriors) or recognize rights of prisoners of war (often slaughtered upon capture), and were disproportionate (in many cases total) in their destruction. (In addition to the wars of conquest in Joshua 6–11, compare the victories of Deborah and Gideon in Judges 4 and 7.) If the Just War tradition spells out for Christians the conditions under which war may be a moral cause, then most of the Israelite wars were clearly immoral; and if immoral, then they provide no precedent for Christian participation in a contemporary Just War.

Fourth, several of the defensive and limited, and hence potentially morally justified, wars in the Old Testament are depicted as being fought by God on Israel's behalf and included no military participation by the Israelites, including the decisive victory at the sea over Pharaoh's army. Israel's role in such wars was simply: "Fear not. Have faith. Be still. And behold the victory of God." God is depicted in such instances as a divine warrior who will defend the Holy Name, the holy people, and the holy city against enemies by divine power alone, using the forces of nature rather than the weapons of humans, the latter of which God destroys (e.g., Exod 14–15; Isa 36–37; Ps 46).[26] Thus, if only ostensibly just wars in the Old Testament may serve as moral precedents for contemporary Christian practice, then there is significant biblical precedent for Christians adopting not only a defensive stance against enemies, but a nonviolent stance that relies not upon the walls and towers of the city, much less the weapons and chariots of the army, but solely upon the promise and power of God.

Fifth, the Old Testament prophets Isaiah and Jeremiah called the Assyrian, Babylonian, and Persian kings God's chosen servants to deal out vengeance and punishment upon Israel and the nations (cf. Isa 10, 45; Jer 25). Isaiah even called Cyrus, king of Persia, God's "anointed" or "messiah" because he was to conquer the Babylonians and thus to liberate the captive Israelites in exile. Such prophetic oracles might be taken as precedents justifying the use of armed force by one nation either to avenge wrongs by another nation (as NATO did in Yugoslavia in 1999) or to impose regime

---

26. For an exploration of this type of Holy War in the Old Testament, see Lind, *Yahweh Is a Warrior*.

Epilogue

change upon a nation with an autocratic, oppressive government (as the United States did in Iraq in 2003).

Notice, however, that according to the prophets these kings that are depicted as instruments of divine wrath are themselves quite ignorant of God's purposes. Cyrus conquers other nations, including Babylon, only to serve his own pride and ambition and his ways are offensive to God (cf. Isa 10:7–11; 48:14–15). Furthermore, each of the Assyrians, Babylonians, and Persians are said by the prophets to be destined themselves for subsequent punishment and defeat by other powers for their pride and violent ways—Assyria by Babylon, Babylon by Persia, Persia by Greece (cf. Isa 10:12ff; 13:1—14:27; Jer 25:12ff.). In sending Persia against Babylon, God is said to "repay Babylon" and "take vengeance" against Nebuchadrezzar, king of Babylon, for the evil he has done not only to Israel but to the other nations he has conquered: "Babylon must fall for the slain of Israel, as the slain of all the earth have fallen because of Babylon" (Jer 51:24, 36, 49). So, while God's sovereign purpose holds sway over the nations, by no means is the prideful violence used by one nation against other nations, even in the cause of vengeance or liberation, thereby justified or acceptable to God. The violence of the nations, no matter how justifiable it may appear to us, cannot escape God's judgment.

In this context it would be useful to reconsider the US Civil War. Many at the time, especially after the Emancipation Proclamation, and since have interpreted that war in biblical terms as a Holy War justified by the cause of liberating the slaves.[27] One might then interpret the Union army as an instrument of divine wrath appointed by God to deal out vengeance upon the South for the evil of slavery, a view expressed in the popular hymn in the North, "The Battle Hymn of the Republic" (1862). Acknowledging the complicity of the entire nation in the legal institution of slavery, however, one might instead interpret the war as a punishment on the nation as a whole. The line between good and evil did not in fact run between North and South, but rather through the heart of every American who gave (even passive) consent to the constitutional system that protected slavery whether they held slaves or not; hence, this war was not one simply of "good versus evil." Indeed, that is just how Abraham Lincoln understood the matter by the end of the war, expressed in his Second Inaugural Address: the war was an atonement in blood for the nation's "original sin," God's judgment upon

---

27. Concerning the contemporary interpretation of the Civil War in theological terms, see Noll, *Civil War*.

Path to Peace—A Disciple's Pilgrimage

the entire nation, not just the South. One might thus say that the Confederate army was just as much an instrument of divine wrath as was the Union army, each repaying the other according to their common transgression—and that the violence of *both* sides was equally *un*acceptable to God, while nonetheless God's sovereign purpose of liberation from slavery held sway over the course of events.[28]

. . . Hitler?

This brings us to the question everyone eventually asks about the way of peace: What about Hitler? Politically, this question gets used and abused to justify questionable wars by making every enemy out to be the incarnation of evil, as George H. W. Bush did regarding Saddam Hussein in 1990 and as George W. Bush did regarding Saddam Hussein in 2002. Nonetheless, it is an inescapable question for Christian disciples if only because of the persistence of egregious evil in our world. To help us address this question, I propose that we consider the following thought experiment.

Suppose we had lived in Paris at the time Hitler's armies were marching into Poland and Austria and across Belgium and the Netherlands and, finally, into France. We are now under occupation by the brutal, oppressive army of a ruthless foreign power. Village after village has been destroyed, our compatriots are being killed by the thousands, and many of our Jewish neighbors are being rounded up and deported to death camps. What shall we do?

What are our options? We could surrender and collaborate with the occupying authority, hoping to save as much of our nation and keep as much control over our affairs and future as we can. That was the choice of the much-despised Vichy regime. We could flee the country to Britain and join the army of the Free French, the remnant in exile that still claims to be the legitimate government of the French republic, hoping to return to France and free it from German occupation by force of arms. We could flee to the countryside of southern France, in hope of escaping the worst of the German military occupation and preserving a little peace for ourselves, waiting for the Allied army to bring liberation. Or we could stay in Paris and fight against the German occupation by joining the ranks of the armed

---

28. For further reflection on war and violence in the Old Testament, see McDonald, *God and Violence*.

Epilogue

underground resistance. Which should we choose? Does this exhaust all of our options?

Now consider this analogy. Were we living in Jerusalem in the early first century, say around 30 AD, we would face a similar choice. For some ninety years now, our country has been occupied by the repressive army of the Roman Empire. We are oppressively taxed and brutally treated. Our villages have been burned, thousands of our compatriots have been executed for resistance, and many of our neighbors have been deported as prisoners and slaves. What shall we do?

What are our options?[29] We could capitulate to Roman rule and collaborate with the provincial governor, hoping to save as much national autonomy as possible and preserve our religious practice within a pagan culture. That was the choice of the Herodians, the chief priests, the Sanhedrin, and the Sadducees. We could join the armed resistance and hide in the hills of Galilee north of Jerusalem, making raids on Roman troop columns and outposts, ambushing the tax collectors and their solider escorts who collaborate with the regime, and waiting for the right moment to liberate Jerusalem by force. That was the choice of the Zealots (and they would liberate Jerusalem by armed insurrection in 66 AD, only to see Jerusalem crushed and the people slaughtered by the Romans four years later). We could flee south to the desert and live an ascetic life, seeking peace and purity in isolation from the political situation, waiting for God to initiate final judgment on both the Roman oppressors and their Jewish collaborators. That was the choice of the Essenes. Or we could remain in Jerusalem and maintain our religious ways all the more strictly to separate ourselves from both the surrounding pagan corruption and the political compromises of our compatriots, but being willing to sacrifice ourselves rather than let the Romans desecrate our holy places. That was the choice of the Pharisees. Which should we choose? Does this exhaust all our options?

As understandable, respectable, and justifiable as each of these choices might appear, Jesus chose none of these ways. He rejected both collaboration and quietism. He insisted on actively engaging the rulers and authorities, but with neither the weapons of armed resistance nor the pragmatism of calculated compromise. While he was closest in philosophy and practice to the Pharisees, Jesus' message and ways set him apart from all the rest (paraphrasing Matt 5):

> Blessed are the meek.

29. The following analysis draws from Yoder, *Original Revolution*.

> Blessed are the merciful.
> Blessed are the peacemakers.
> Blessed are those who are persecuted for the sake of righteousness.
>
> You have heard it said, "An eye for an eye." But I say to you, do not resist evil with evil. But instead if a Roman authority hits you on the right cheek, turn the other also. And if a Roman soldier forces you to walk one mile, go also the second mile.
>
> You have heard it said, "Love your neighbor and hate your enemy." But I say to you, Love your enemies and pray for the Roman occupiers who persecute and oppress you. In that way you will be children of your Father in Heaven.
>
> Love everyone, therefore, as your heavenly Father loves the righteous and the wicked, the good and the evil, alike.

As a Christian disciple, this is my confession: I believe that the best answer to the question, What about Hitler?—the answer having the first and strongest claim on my loyalty and allegiance, the answer that best conforms to the ways and purposes of God's kingdom—is precisely the same answer that Jesus himself taught and lived in the face of the question, What about Rome?

The imperatives of the Sermon on the Mount—"Love your enemies. Do not return evil for evil. Bless those who curse you. Pray for those who harm you."—do not have the character of abstract moral commands intuited by the ideal rational agent. Nor are they legalistic "oughts" imposed as if from nowhere and lacking in personal motivation. Instead, they have the character of "therefore" and "so that." They are *invitations* motivated by God's grace and rooted in trust in God's promise: Through Christ, God has redeemed you from death and freed you from fear; *therefore*, in response to this grace and by the power of the Holy Spirit, trust in God's promise to deliver you from evil, do God's will and love as God loves, *so that* you may share now in the blessings of God's peaceable kingdom to come. A crucial caveat must be added here: the "Jesus option" is not for everyone, but only for disciples—those who have entrusted their physical security to the providence of an all-wise God, yielded their inner lives to the transforming power of the interceding Spirit, and committed their whole selves to following the risen Jesus. The kingdom ethic is thus normatively compelling only for the discipleship community of redeemed believers. Even though Jesus has been exalted by God as Lord of the nations (Phil 2) and will judge the nations according to their deeds (Matt 25), those who have not been regenerated by God's grace through the Holy Spirit cannot be expected to live out the kingdom ethic taught by Jesus. Instead, the word of the Christian to the non-Christian is, as it has always been, repent and be converted: "we entreat you on behalf of Christ, be reconciled to God" (2 Cor 5:20).

Now, the "Jesus option" is not just a pious ideal of moral perfection, impossible and irrelevant in a fallen, sinful world.[30] In fact, faithful Christians have actually practiced what Jesus taught, even amidst the hellish reign of the Third Reich. During the Nazi occupation of France during World War Two, the Protestant (Huguenot) village of Le Chambon, led by local minister André Trocme, addressed the evil situation around them with suffering service and nonviolent resistance, seeking to overcome evil with good in the manner of Christ. In defiance of the Nazi occupation policy, the Christians of Le Chambon made their village a safe haven for Jews threatened with deportation and extermination. Villagers opened their homes to Jewish neighbors and refugees to save them from destruction, thus exposing themselves to risk of arrest and imprisonment or deportation. Trocmé himself was arrested and interrogated in an internment camp for several weeks.[31] This episode serves as an enduring witness by and to the church—a witness both to costly fidelity to the way of Jesus and to possibilities realizable by the power of the Spirit.

---

30. Such was the view of Niebuhr, *Interpretation of Christian Ethics*. For a critique of Niebuhr's view, see my book, *Atonement, Justice, and Peace*, 560–72.

31. Hallie, *Lest Innocent Blood Be Shed*.

Bibliography

Ackerman, Peter, and Jack Duvall. *A Force More Powerful: A Century of Nonviolent Conflict*. New York: Palgrave, 2000.
Amstutz, Jim. *Threatened with Resurrection: Self-Preservation and Christ's Way of Peace*. Scottdale, PA: Herald, 2002.
Aquinas, Thomas. *Summa Theologiae*. Excerpted in *War and Christian Ethics: Classical Readings on the Morality of War*, edited by Arthur F. Holmes, 92–117. Grand Rapids: Baker, 1975.
Arnold, Eberhard. *Salt and Light: Living the Sermon on the Mount*, 4th ed. Farmington, PA: Plough, 1998.
Arnold, J. Heinrich. *Discipleship: Living for Christ in the Daily Grind*. Farmington, PA: Plough, 1994.
Augustine. *City of God*. Excerpted in *The Problem of Evil: Selected Readings*, edited by Michael L. Peterson, 191–96. Notre Dame, IN: University of Notre Dame Press, 1992.
———. *Reply to Faustus the Manichean*. Excerpted in *War and Christian Ethics: Classical Readings on the Morality of War*, edited by Arthur F. Holmes, 63–68. Grand Rapids: Baker, 1975.
Bainton, Roland H. *Christian Attitudes toward War and Peace: A Historical Survey and Critical Re-evaluation*. Nashville: Abingdon, 1960.
Barrett, Gregg. *The Gospel of Rutba: War, Peace, and the Good Samaritan Story in Iraq*. Maryknoll, NY: Orbis, 2012.
Bonhoeffer, Dietrich. *The Cost of Discipleship*. Rev. ed. New York: MacMillan, 1959.
The Book of Common Prayer. N.p.: Seabury, 1979.
Brueggemann, Walter. *The Prophetic Imagination*, 2nd ed. Minneapolis: Fortress, 2001.
Camus, Albert. *The Plague*. Translated by Stuart Gilbert. 1948. New York: Random House, 1972.
Cassidy, Richard J. *John's Gospel in New Perspective: Christology and the Realities of Roman Power*. Maryknoll, NY: Orbis, 1992.
Claiborne, Shane. *The Irresistible Revolution: Living as an Ordinary Radical*. Grand Rapids: Zondervan, 2006.
Coble, Ann Louise. *Cotton Patch for the Kingdom: Clarence Jordan's Demonstration Plot at Koinonia Farm*. Scottdale, PA: Herald, 2002.
Day, Dorothy. *The Long Loneliness*. New York: Harper & Row, 1952.
Dostoevsky, Fyodor. *The Brothers Karamazov*. Translated by Andrew H. MacAndrew. 1970. Toronto: Bantam, 1981.
Early Christian Writings. Translated by Maxwell Staniforth. London: Penguin, 1987.
Elshtain, Jean Bethke. *Just War against Terror: The Burden of American Power in a Violent World*. New York: Basic Books, 2003.

Bibliography

Fry, Timothy O.S.B. *The Rule of Saint Benedict in Latin and English with Notes.* Collegeville, MN: Liturgical, 1981.

Gish, Arthur G. *Hebron Journal: Stories of Nonviolent Peacemaking.* Scottdale, PA: Herald, 2001.

Greenberg, Moshe. "The Biblical Grounding of Human Value." In *The Samuel Friedland Lectures, 1960-1966*, 39–51. New York: Jewish Theological Seminary, 1966.

Gregory of Nazianzus. *On God and Man: The Theological Poetry of St. Gregory of Nazianzus.* Translated by Peter Gilbert. Crestwood, NY: St. Vladimir's Seminary Press, 2001.

Hallie, Phillip P. *Lest Innocent Blood Be Shed: The Story of Le Chambon and How Goodness Happened There.* New York: Harper & Row, 1979.

Holmes, Arthur F. *War and Christian Ethics: Classical Readings on the Morality of War.* Grand Rapids: Baker, 1975.

Hornus, Jean-Michel. *It Is Not Lawful for Me to Fight: Early Christian Attitudes Toward War, Violence, and the State.* Scottdale, PA: Herald, 1980.

Horsley, Richard A. *Jesus and Empire: The Kingdom of God and the New World Disorder.* Minneapolis: Fortress, 2003.

Human Rights Watch. *Civilian Deaths in the NATO Air Campaign.* New York: Human Rights Watch, 2000.

———. *Needless Deaths in the Gulf War: Civilian Casualties during the Air Campaign and Violations of the Laws of War.* New York: Human Rights Watch, 1991.

Hume, John. *Personal Views: Politics, Peace and Reconciliation in Ireland.* Middlesex: Roberts Rinehart, 1996.

Jones, Douglas M. *Dismissing Jesus: How We Evade the Way of the Cross.* Eugene, OR: Cascade, 2013.

Juhnke, James C., and Carol M. Hunter. *The Missing Peace: The Search for Nonviolent Alternatives in United States History.* Kitchener, ON: Pandora, 2001.

Kenny, John P. *Chaosmos.* Unpublished.

Klaassen, Walter. *Anabaptism in Outline: Selected Primary Sources.* Waterloo, ON: Herald, 1981.

Kraybill, Donald, and Linda Gehman Peachey. *Where Was God on September 11? Seeds of Faith and Hope.* Scottdale, PA: Herald, 2002.

Kreider, Alan, Eleanor Kreider, and Paulus Widjaja. *A Culture of Peace: God's Vision for the Church.* Intercourse, PA: Good Books, 2005.

Lind, Millard C. *Yahweh Is a Warrior: The Theology of Warfare in Ancient Israel.* Scottdale, PA: Herald, 1980.

Luther, Martin. "Whether Soldiers, Too, Can Be Saved." Excerpted in *War and Christian Ethics: Classical Readings on the Morality of War*, edited by Arthur F. Holmes, 140–64. Grand Rapids: Baker, 1975.

Marshall, Christopher D. *Beyond Retribution: A New Testament Vision for Justice, Crime, and Punishment.* Grand Rapids: Eerdmans, 2001.

Mauser, Ulrich. *The Gospel of Peace: A Scriptural Message for Today's World.* Louisville: Westminster John Knox, 1992.

McDonald, Patricia M. *God and Violence: Biblical Resources for Living in a Small World.* Scottdale, PA: Herald, 2004.

Merton, Thomas. *The Seven Storey Mountain.* San Diego: Harcourt Brace, 1948.

Mosley, Don. *With Our Own Eyes: The Dramatic Story of a Christian Response to the Wounds of War, Racism, and Oppression.* Scottdale, PA: Herald, 1996.

Bibliography

Mykolaitis-Putinas, Vincas. "Pensive Christ by the Roadside" (1926). In *Voices of Lithuanian Poetry*, 40–43. Translated by Lionginas Pazusis. Vilnius: Tyto Alba, 2001.

Nassar, David. "Palestinians who are working toward peace." *The Christian Science Monitor*, March 4 (2003).

Niditch, Susan. *War in the Hebrew Bible: A Study in the Ethics of Violence*. Oxford: Oxford University Press, 1993.

Niebuhr, Reinhold. *An Interpretation of Christian Ethics*. New York: Meridian, 1958.

———. "Why the Christian Church Is not Pacifist." In *War and Christian Ethics: Classical Readings on the Morality of War*, edited by Arthur F. Holmes, 301–13. Grand Rapids: Baker, 1975.

Noll, Mark A. *The Civil War as a Theological Crisis*. Chapel Hill, NC: The University of North Carolina Press, 2006.

Nouwen, Henri J. M., Donald P. McNeill, and Douglas A. Morrison. *Compassion: A Reflection on the Christian Life*. New York: Doubleday, 1983.

Philpott, Daniel. *Just and Unjust Peace: An Ethic of Political Reconciliation*. New York: Oxford University Press, 2012.

Rensberger, David. *Johannine Faith and Liberating Community*. Philadelphia: Westminster, 1988.

Rilke, Ranier Maria. *Rilke's Book of Hours: Love Poems to God*. Translated by Anita Barrows and Joanna Macy. New York: Riverhead, 1996.

Roth, John D. *Choosing Against War: A Christian View*. Intercourse, PA: Good Books, 2002.

Saldarini, Anthony J. *Pharisees, Scribes and Sadducees in Palestinian Society: A Sociological Approach*. Wilmington, DE: Michael Glazier, 1988.

Snyder, C. Arnold. *The Life and Thought of Michael Sattler*. Scottdale, PA: Herald, 1984.

Snyder Belousek, Darrin W. *Atonement, Justice, and Peace: The Message of the Cross and the Mission of the Church*. Grand Rapids: Eerdmans, 2012.

———. *Good News: The Advent of Salvation in the Gospel of Luke*. Collegeville, MN: Liturgical, 2014.

———. "'Has Christ been divided? Was Paul crucified for you?' The evangelical imperative of ecumenical peacemaking and the Bridgefolk (Mennonite-Catholic) movement." *Mennonite Life* 62 (2007). Online: http://mennonitelife.bethelks.edu/2013/07/has-christ-been-divided-was-paul-crucified-for-you-vol-62-no-2/.

———. "How can the battle be won? War rhetoric makes false assumptions about good, evil." *Mennonite Weekly Review*, 10 March (2003) 4.

———. "Is Jesus Lord?" In *Where was God on September 11? Seeds of Faith and Hope*, edited by Donald B. Kraybill and Linda G. Peachey, 57–59. Scottdale, PA: Herald, 2002.

———. "The Meeting of Body, Spirit, and Soil: A Kingdom Parable." *DreamSeeker Magazine*, 5 (Autumn 2005) 43–46.

———. "Pacifists have duty to be nation's conscience." *Mennonite Weekly Review*, 23 September (2002) 6.

———. "Service and Sacrifice." *The Mennonite*, July (2010). Online: http://www.themennonite.org/issues/13-7/articles/Service_and_sacrifice_even_vacations.

———. "Surprised by joy: A personal story of Advent." *The Mennonite*, December (2011) 22–24. Online: http://www.themennonite.org/issues/14-12/articles/Surprised_by_Joy.

Bibliography

———. "Thinking clearly about abortion." *The Mennonite*, 5 August (2003) 18. Online: http://www.themennonite.org/pdf/magazine_pdf_57.pdf.

———. "Thinking clearly about abortion, again." *The Mennonite*, February (2010) 60. Online:http://www.themennonite.org/issues/13-2/articles/Thinking_clearly_about_abortion_again.

———. "Toward a Consistent Ethic of Life in the Peace Tradition Perspective: A Critical-Constructive Response to the MC USA Statement on Abortion." *Mennonite Quarterly Review* 79 (2005) 439–80.

———. "Tragic zeal: The spiral of violence, vengeance and death." *The Mennonite*, 7 September (2004) 16–17. Online: http://www.themennonite.org/attachments/pdfs/0000/0072/Issue17-7.pdf.

Sprinkle, Preston. *Fight: A Christian Case for Nonviolence*. Colorado Springs: David C. Cook, 2013.

Stoner, André Gingerich. "The Death Penalty: A Church's Growing Response." In *MCC Washington Memo*, vol. XXXIII, no. 5 (September–October 2001). Online: http://washingtonmemo.files.wordpress.com/2009/12/memo_01_5.pdf.

Surin, Kenneth. "Taking Suffering Seriously." In *The Problem of Evil: Selected Readings*, edited by Michael L. Peterson, 339–49. Notre Dame, IN: University of Notre Dame Press, 1992.

Swartley, Willard M. *Covenant of Peace: The Missing Peace in New Testament Theology and Ethics*. Grand Rapids: Eerdmans, 2006.

Swoboda, Jörg. *The Revolution of the Candles: Christians in the Revolution of the German Democratic Republic*. Macon, GA: Mercer University Press, 1996.

Vanier, Jean. *Drawn into the Mystery of Jesus through the Gospel of John*. Ottawa: Novalis, 2004.

Weil, Simone. *Waiting for God*. New York: Harper & Row, 1973.

Wiesel, Elie. *Night*. Translated by Stella Rodway. 1960. New York: Bantam, 1982.

Wink, Walter. *Engaging the Powers: Discernment and Resistance in a World of Domination*. Minneapolis: Fortress, 1992.

Yoder, John Howard. *He Came Preaching Peace*. Scottdale, PA: Herald, 1985.

———. *Nevertheless: The Varieties and Shortcomings of Religious Pacifism*, rev. and exp. edition. Scottdale, PA: Herald, 1992.

———. *The Original Revolution: Essays on Christian Pacifism*. Scottdale, PA: Herald, 1971.

———. *The Politics of Jesus*. Grand Rapids: Eerdmans, 1972.

———. *What Would You Do? A Serious Answer to a Standard Question*. Exp. ed. Scottdale, PA: Herald, 1992.

———. *When War Is Unjust: Being Honest in Just-War Thinking*, 2nd ed. Maryknoll, NY: Orbis, 1996.

Yoder, Perry B. *Shalom: The Bible's Word for Salvation, Justice, and Peace*. Nappanee, IN: Evangel, 1987.

www.ingramcontent.com/pod-product-compliance
Lightning Source LLC
Chambersburg PA
CBHW031433150426
43191CB00006B/493